LIBRARIANSHIP
Redefining and Redesigning Beyond the Customary Craft

LIBRARIANSHIP

Redefining and Redesigning Beyond the Customary Craft

By
Shiva Sukula

Ess Ess Publications
New Delhi

LIBRARIANSHIP
Redefining and Redesigning Beyond the Customary Craft

ISBN: 978-81-7000-805-7

First Published 2016

Published by:
Ess Ess Publications
4831/24, Ansari Road,
Darya Ganj,
New Delhi-110 002.
INDIA
Phones: 23260807, 41563444
Fax: 41563334
E-mail: info@essessreference.com
www.essessreference.com

Cover Design by *Patch Creative Unit*

Printed and bound in India at Salasar Imaging Systems.

Contents

Foreword

As higher education system in India has evolved through recent decades, academic libraries have not prepared themselves accordingly to meet the challenges to serve faculty & students more effectively. Academic and research libraries in changing time need to adopt digital technologies and also need to provide training in the use of these technologies to both staff and users. Academic libraries are a hub of education in an academic institution. As rightly stated by none other than former President of India Late Dr. S. Radhakrishnan, that Library is as the heart of an academic institution. Dr. S. R. Ranganathan has also defined importance of a library by mentioning it as the trinity of Library staff, users (faculty & students) and resources.

The basic objectives of an academic library today are almost same as in past. However, the role and functions of an academic library now have vastly changed. The means and medium of the collection of resources, its organization, tools to analyze it, and means of dissemination, all are now technology driven. Remote access technologies are helpful in providing anytime anywhere access, because of that users are having options; to visit a library or may not. Federated search and web scale discovery technologies are helping libraries in providing Google-like search to both in-house resources as well as subscribed contents. Due to such developments there is a stronger need to re-define the present role of libraries and librarians and also to re-design services according to the current needs of the users.

This book by Dr. Shiva Shukla is an attempt to present an overview of the new and emerging form of librarianship that may be referred as Embedded Librarianship. During last four years, Central Library, JNU has undergone a systematic transformation from a traditional academic library to one of the most modern academic library. This transformation at JNU has converted Central Library, JNU from a resource centre to a customer focused service organization. Due to my preoccupation in hosting ETD 2015: International Symposium on Electronic Theses and Dissertations" being held during November 04-06, 2015 at Convention Centre, Jawaharlal Nehru University, New Delhi, I did not have much opportunity to go through the entire contents of the book. However as per my understanding, the author has made an attempt to redefine the new role of academic libraries by presenting the story of re-engineering process at Central Library, JNU. The author has also provided a systematic and innovative approach towards redesigning a modern academic library. She has also touched upon various issues concerning new and innovative library services for academic libraries.

I understand the book might be useful to academic, and research libraries particularly to those who are in the process of redesigning and renovation, and are looking for guidelines in these areas, and in general to all academic libraries. These libraries may learn from the experience of Central Library, JNU. The students and researchers in the field of library and information science may also find it useful for furthering the area of their research.

To close, may I express the appreciation and admiration, for the extraordinary efforts of Author by bringing out a volume of this kind within less than one year of her joining in JNU

Dr. Ramesh C Gaur

PGDCA, MLISc, Ph.D. Fulbright Scholar (Virginia Tech, USA)
University Librarian, Jawaharlal Nehru University (JNU)
Email: rcgaur@mail.jnu.ac.in; rcgaur66@gmail.com

Preface

The librarianship gives wings to the overview of a responsible, service-oriented and not-for-profit culture in the organization. Various kinds of organizations emphasize on the strong library in terms of collection, services and sustainability in each aspect that matters for the entire system. The leadership is inherent in librarianship while dealing with issues such as financial planning, human resource management, and using technologies in an academic library. Library management involves intricately related with housekeeping functions such as acquisition, periodical management, technical processing, and various others including resource sharing. Apart from these functions, the modern library management requirements such as licensing the e-resources, electronic cataloguing and metadata services, use of web-based classification systems, and interlibrary loan especially for the e-books are few of the complex component tasks in the library.

The discovery of information from the millions of records is not possible unless the designing of information system has taken place in such a way that explains all the answers from the information quest. The digital collection management has emerged in the form of a new area of concern. The library readers are interested in Virtual Reference as well as web-based information gateway. The librarianship is moving towards the library management and services placed on the platforms of open source and open access. The comprehensiveness and global characteristics of knowledge requirements are based on networked information solutions. The library users are becoming partners in collection building and the librarians are building 'tools' to create innovation in the libraries. In the times of myriad formats and standards for every information item in library, it is difficult to manage the content and provide. The tools like EZproxy, discovery services and trainings are supportive in efficient services. The challenges that academic libraries are facing are bigger than the imaginations and earlier than expectations if the focus is shifted towards the lack of funds, inappropriate financial planning, rapidly changing information environment and pressures of modernity in context with information and communication technologies (ICTs). The academic library has taken the form of a learning center where the whispers are hidden and buzz is around. The learning opportunities created by library emerge in the shape of events for training, author workshops etc. The introduction of a flexible modern approach under the guided principles of librarianship paves way for efficient and innovative library and information services.

The present book displays the panoramic journey of an academic library according under the leading librarianship. During the recently passed years, there have been various developments in the library practices due to the factors such as ICT, library and information tools, research supporting tools and techniques at Central Library, Jawaharlal Nehru University (JNU Library). The gradual as well as sudden changes in the library environment have been depicted in the chapters framed in this book. The prologue introduces about the library and the Epilogue leads towards futuristic aspirations in the academic library. In between, the chapters roll out to present the advancement of JNU library in a way that reflects the sequence of development, progress and sustainability. The contents in the forms of these chapters provide an example to carry on the legacy as well as modernity in each facet that builds a good academic library. The discussions in the book are the reflections of the inspired librarianship. The intricate facets of library are discussed to inform about the dynamically designed information environment and the developments taken place during last couple of years. The embedding librarianship has been displayed in the chapters through the independent yet interrelated concepts; and the practices going on in the Central Library, Jawaharlal Nehru University, New Delhi. The facets and formats of librarianship are discussed in a manner that provides a vast range of contemporary elements as well as the characteristics of futurism.

— Shiva Sukula

1
Prologue
History but not Mystery

About the past of library and how the librarianship was existing at this place. The picture in conventional frame!

The libraries are the knowledge hubs and learning centers since the ancient times when few civilizations were grooming themselves. The making of states or countries in very early phases of world history are filled with the stories of libraries and the kings visiting them though not meant for general public. What the current humankind visualizes is the legacy of libraries as supporter in learning, leisurely reading and few more functions that are carrying the social or community building. While initiating the discussion about one of the prominent library (academic library) of India, the name of Central Library, Jawaharlal Nehru University, New Delhi is well-known and serving the users in the best possible way.

If the times are recalled, the key elements of learning are always similar though centuries have passed. And comparison of various libraries at various time-frames gives a picture of varied administrative structure and procedures, inclusion of subjects or proliferation of disciplines due to growing nature of research or the way the human resources in the libraries are developed. The faint memories from the past support the creation of current glimpse of libraries' development. The spiraling development is overwhelming if the necessities of generation wise progress of any library are compassed.

The developments are not "in-one-go" kind of steps during couple of decades where the libraries have reappeared before its people in a highly dramatic frame and outlook. The contexts of development can be found in the contemporary education scenario, worldwide revolution of information and communication technologies and of course the willingness of the librarianship itself. There are few controversies over the progress made by libraries yet the concurrent river of libraries and their panoramic journey is full of surprises.

So introducing the Central Library of Jawaharlal Nehru University as kind of the old academic library, post-independence, it was established in 1969. It has been functioning as "Knowledge Centre" since last five-six decades. It is rich in diversity of collections which belong to Sciences, Humanities and Social Sciences. The vast building of library houses vast collections of literature in various languages which are rare in nature and special to have been collected. As far as the carpet –area of library is concerned, it is having approximately one lakh sq. ft. floor to keep running the journey of library and its collection alive over the big number of years. The nine-story building is a huge complex to house a university library. The library has many kinds of documents in its collection; these are books (print as well as electronic), journal in print and digital form, research reports, microforms and Government data documents.

Looking into history, it is reiterated that the initial library incorporated the prestigious Indian School of International Studies Library. This library merged with the then established library of Jawaharlal Nehru University. The

JNU Library functions as depository library of all Govt. publications. In its special collection, it includes the publications of various important International Organizations such as WHO and UN. The readers can easily find documents related with European Union, United Nations and its allied agencies etc. The nine-storey building forms a huge tower which is the tallest in the university campus. The beautiful hills of Aravali and greenery surround the library which make this library and its ambience a welcoming space to its readers.

The objectives of the JNU library like any other kind of library include the function to serve its readers. The users of library are always taught how to use library but an academic library like JNU library has few specific aims such as procuring, organizing and disseminating the contained information in various formats as and when required by the users. It supports library services in order to promote the use of rich collection along with preservation of the legacy that it is carrying. It has created a learning environment to support the teaching and learning objectives of the faculty members, researchers, and students. It serves not only those who work or study at the campus but also those who are affiliated or visit from other organizations and institutions. The objectives of the library encompass certain elements which are very significant in terms of readers' services. How intricately; the user satisfaction, their needs and services are interwoven, is an outcome of planned and phased development of this library.

CONCERNS OF LIBRARY: FEW FACETS AND RELATIONS

The library has been concerned with the issues such as developing a general collection or including specialized ones; having a sole responsibility of faculty members for collection development or inclusion of each component of 'academic ecology' in this activity or moving towards the modernization of services. The presence of an administrative duty or a managerial function may also require attention in relation with the spirit of running the library also on debating over the compartmentalized library administration and management. The integrity of library is composed of various simultaneous plans put into actions. The feasibility of actions and the restructuring of plans are always before the library authorities and leadership yet the challenges are overcome with the sound planning and policies.

The enthusiasm of library staff as well as the fears of not coping with fast pacing technologies may be few of the aspects with which the JNU library has always been concerned. The organizational expansion, increasing number of enrollments and the faculty members in ratio to that are not separate from the challenges before the library where the knowledge explosion is the biggest challenge. The recent times have witnessed the accommodation of interdisciplinary research and the related collection development yet the conclusions cannot be drawn on the basis of current scenario. The burgeoned issues of innovative services have been a combination of users' needs and expectations.

THE LEARNING AND THE LIBRARY INSTRUCTIONS

The vast amount of information is a challenge for the collection development aspect. This is faced by the reader or searcher in the library also in context with how to find authentic information or use the maximum number of resources on a given topic or the documents available in a given subject. The users face the dilemma how to find out the most relevant sources and access them. Libraries are near to the solution by providing them federated search engines and attractive web interfaces, but the question of access to all resources in a limited period of time always creeps before the library and its user. JNU library has been concerned with this problem at the core, and it has found the solution though a matter of time limit is difficult to be overcome. The efforts at individual user's level are always needed to be exercised. Various attempt to instruct the readers about identifying, locating and accessing the information resources are always required due to changing nature of formats and users' demand as well. The library orientation, user education and resources awareness programs are needed throughout the year and JNU library has been endeavoring to let the users reach their needed resources at the earliest. The inclusion of various electronic resources and their associated terms and conditions such as copyright, fair use and the licensing aspects force the library to keep the user informed for guided use of these electronic resources.

ASSUMPTIONS AND APPROACHES

It is difficult to find out the consensus over a range of problems and planning yet the approaches are comprehensive and pinpointed problems at the same time. There is need of practical means and methods to have basic solutions and to cope with the expectations of library users. The repetition and reiterating of the users' problems is similar for academic libraries. To rescue the library staff from such situations, an explicit approach and well-framed action plan is needed. To have sizable amount of output from the deliberations the choice of those alternatives is required that are feasible and attainable. The conformity with the organizational policies and development direction is significant in order to move in rhythm. The widespread general picture of lack of resources or funds in libraries needs to be changed and diverted when there are options of open source and open access area available. The slim chances of usability of various cost-free approaches provide hope to libraries in the era when the funds are crunching and staff is reduced to few numbers. To introduce specialized resources and services subscribe to the idea of innovation. To have less mechanical yet flexible system is need of the hour. When the readers want quality-based resources and an ambience that is user friendly, the academic library is compelled and motivated as well, to have advanced levels of services.

The rationale for library development is measured in means of the popularity of the same among the users. The useful thought for the progress of library originates and forms an essential attribute to its collection, services and ability to sustain over a period of time. The obsolescence is another aspect that always troubles any library in context with collection and infrastructure. The plausible proposition has been in the form of articulation of present day situations before the library with a projection of futuristic approach in terms of conceptual enterprise. To produce the underpinnings for an academic library, what needed is sufficient investment of time and action. The question arises if any of these are available in plenty when the technology gets older by tomorrow and obsolete by day after tomorrow. To accomplish the role of a model library in academic perspectives, the parallel growth and more interest in library are supposed to do well.

To overcome the past practices or any aspect that may picture a conventional image of library needs speculation as to avoid confrontation between the modernity and traditional library practices. The intriguing facets are the library staff, introduction of fast changing technologies and a mindset which is entirely opposite of what was being carried from the long ago past.

ORGANIZATIONAL STRUCTURE, CULTURE AND SCULPTURE

The drastic changes in the academic environment led to lay down new foundations for achievements and further targets. The augmented usage of online resources and the cumbersome processes in academic pursuits have also compelled the library to evaluate the ongoing processes that were components of usual library routine. The apparent abilities and the complexity of information environment are highly concerned with the structure and culture of JNU academic. The changing environment has influenced the policy makers and authorities to bring out the altered sculpture at JNU. The competencies and challenges were made face to face to find out a ventricle for the highly pressurized information environment.

To achieve the maximum objectives, the library needed to transform itself into a hub of learning apart from being a service organization. The arguments refer to new positions that have been taken by library during recent years. The ceaseless supply of electronic resources and print documents in abundance has conditionally inferred upon to move towards the learning enterprise. The changing conditions have contributed in akin to previously set goals to serve the readers keeping in view the instructional role of library staff. Whereas the readers are habitual of fast modifications in the library services, the habituation comes handy while bringing them towards the new roles of library. The library has found a new relation in the form of "tutorial one". There are no chances when the library finds itself to an achieved position, once the target are met at an appreciable degree, there is no substitution of the services and commitments related with library users. The enhancement of library performance is always to be achieved with the introduction of new objectives and services. The sharp focus of the library always remains on the organizational, academic and research goal. The added expense of service leads to expansion of enlightenment in the library as well as JNU.

Various Schools Library Centers at JNU

1. Centre for Historical Studies

2. Centre for Political Studies
3. Centre for Studies in Science Policy
4. School of Social Sciences
5. Centre for Women's Studies
6. Centre for Social Medicine & Community Health
7. School of Computer and Systems Sciences
8. School of Arts and Aesthetics
9. School of Biotechnology
10. School of Computational and Integrative Sciences
11. School of Life Sciences

Various schools and centers have these well-focused libraries which are boon to students. Some of these libraries are the outcomes of the documents, books acquired during running of various research projects. The time and diversity in research progress have been instrumental in the developing of richness in the collections available at these libraries.

THE GENESIS AND GOALS

The modern library is all about the information access and information services. The librarianship as a profession connects people to the sources of knowledge. The soul of this profession lies in the offer of service in various areas such as educational, organizational, industrial, and many more. The vibrancy of library depends on the up to date infrastructure, well-trained staff and the enthusiasm of innovation. Academic libraries reflect keenness in making arrangement to let the academic community reach to every document acquired for the library collection. The significance of strategic actions open up new vista in library management, and innovative services.

The advanced technologies, research support tools, and the necessity to reach widest audience have forced the academic libraries to search the mechanisms and apply the best method to achieve the user satisfaction. The jobs and responsibilities of librarian and library staff in a modern library involves entire bunch of tasks that relate to customers' expectations and services. From borrowing books to accessing e-resources, there are many purposes for the library visitors. To enhance accessibility, the card catalogues are replaced by online public access catalogues (OPACs) along with the marketing of information sources and services.

The perceptions made earlier twenty-thirty years back are being altered due to the interwoven nature of information technology and librarianship. The changing methods of library-user communications in the light of email lists, blogs, and social media feeds are great tools to overcome the communication-barriers. The newer information-related areas like human-computer interaction are envisioning the library services. It has become an important need to create awareness among the prospective and potential users by maximizing the visibility of library resources, offering the information services, and providing the platforms where the users can help themselves for using the resources. The demands, choices, and abundance of electronic resources have created an environment for better access.

Due to the digital revolution the role of libraries has emerged in stronger manner in order to inform, identify and provide authentic information. The perplexed users come to library to explore the vast collection of various kinds of information resources which are available in the form of printed and electronic books, printed and electronic journals; databases; electronic theses and myriad kinds of documents. The range of services provided by the academic libraries reflects the variety and diversity in the roles of library. The canvass of librarianship especially in the academic library is filled with constantly changing colors of users' needs, availability of technologies, tools and information. The changing times are showing a bit different picture of library in the form of becoming a place of learning with interaction, enhancing the community building by collaboration.

What we visualize is the continuous change in the educational environment especially in higher education. The libraries devoted to academic organizations particularly in university systems are overburdened and crowded with newer strategies. The multitudes of processes, steps and component strategies need to be simplified to deal with the increasing number of students, and library services. The growth and maturity in the academic community has motivated the library to improve the processes and excel the outcomes. The user community needs the painless access to the library resources. The easy access and solutions to information needs are the 'must' delivery from an academic library. The syndicated process of searching the library resources expedites the visibility and access. The trouble-shooting followed by a feedback provides glimpses into the ongoing problems. The wide array of resources need the visibility and the users need the visibility of information resources by inter library loan also. The library needs to update the workflows in order to meet the users' expectations and needs.

2

The Librarianship in an Academic Library

From a far Place, Envisioned the Golden Horizon

About the librarianship and plans for JNU library! What was the outlook in mind that was to be grown up here?

INTRODUCTION

The strategic shift takes place in every area of development, without losing its shine towards libraries. In the past the libraries were the place "to do" something for the users now have a role "to urge and enable" the users. The concentration discerns in the understanding of capable technologies and 'crating' an ambience for the library staff to deliver. The redefining and researching have been the core components of emerged librarianship. Discerning the last couple of years, the library as an organization has gone through following transformations:

- Providing opportunities for the electronic methods of knowing the fresh events such as news e-clippings.
- Continuous restructuring and reconfiguring the

physical space as well as collections emphasizing the need of new storage mediums and providing information at various sitting places.

- Inducing the knowledge of providing services and using resources with the support of technology and modern equipments.
- Optimizing the research and relations with users as Library- Faculty collaborations to influence the users in their required way.
- Developing services and content digitally using the latest technologies to provide the customized answers for the specific demands of users. The platforms such as websites, library portals, social media etc. have emerged to bring the users towards the library and vice-versa.
- Breaking the cobwebs of traditional roles of library and inputting the observations in library services; understanding the users; creation of content and services to meet the goals of organization.

How library has evolved is a matter of further observation and discussion as follows:

i. Provision of licensed electronic content and access to the library users within and outside the library, thus removing the physical barrier.

ii. Convert the library into an active destination though the facility of "remote login" is available, by the means of electronic communication and social media tools.

iii. Creating modes for "deliverance of digital content" by migrating to the digital sources and including sophisticated search tools and mechanisms.

iv. Identifying and implementing a 'single search platform' to provide users accessing entire reservoir of knowledge by a single click.

Developing the customer centric environment by training, engaging and embedding the staff in newly evolved services and making them learn to understand the difficult demands of library users beyond specificity of words or search strategy; has been a single motto.

THE DREAMS IN LIBRARIANSHIP AND ACADEMIC LIBRARY USERS

i. Access to all : The first motto generates the basic idea of library and librarianship. In "All" the resources and users are comprised. Here the laws of Dr. S. R. Ranganathan present the image of every user being served with the maximum utilization of present resources in the library. Since the last millennium, the electronic or digital mode has proven to serve this very basic objective of any academic library. The stewardship a library has bestowed in protecting, managing and providing the sources of library has enormously changed. The libraries are involved in creating access to the content scattered worldwide through subscription and Inter Library Loan.

The implementation of federated search and option of print plus electronic has helped the library in creating more opportunities and saving the time as well as space. Certainly the licensing options let emerge few lines on the forehead yet their availability on the devices fulfills the desired use by the library users.

The means of deliverance without or without much-restrictions open a new vista of increased use of electronic content in library.

ii. Special collections to Specific Readers : The recommended books, the suggested titles are among the most or often used collections but libraries have 'special collections' less used yet the precious component of libraries. To make that collection read by the users' needs few efforts such creating awareness, visibility, accessibility and also informing the value of 'special collection'. Here the digitization proves to be helpful in preservation as well as fulfilling the goals mentioned in previous statement. The procedural steps are as following:

a. Digitizing such collections.

b. The awareness by topics relevant to users' search.

- Highlighting the suitability for special occasions, organizational goals or specific academic events.
- Creation and embedment of special collection in routine workflow of library.
- Providing access by the provisions of database, website and searchable by subject, location etc. by having an e-index for the same.
- Taking care of licensing, social media awareness and tools to create curiosity and generate a buzz at affordable cost.

iii. Finding the suitable medium to reach to users : With the help of suitable library services, the users can be reached. The use of 'virtual' services, social media with customized programming; and focus on contextual research to integrate the users in design and implementation have been specialized areas of concern. The transformation of reference services or communicating the users is visible when compared to former forms of services.

The altered mechanisms of trainings, content provisions and concepts of 'self-service' in library have converted the shape of library services. The inclusion of high-end applications in managing the digital resources and services has become need of the survival for the academic libraries. How fast the young generation wants the information is the motivating and guiding factor for the library. The learning capacity of students cannot be ignored when it comes to use new gadgets, devices or platforms.

The designing of new services are based on certain electronic inclinations including the following factors:

- To embed the library staff with the users' groups, function collaboratively with the technology and find out the funding from external sources also.
- To work in close connection of technology, exchanging instructions, training, and knowledge of technology transfer.
- To design e-based reference services with the view of global reference, and expert reference service.
- Increased and enhanced inclusion of online tools, and strategies for on-demand individual centric services.
- To support services by a single platform yet use of multiple channels such as OPAC, library website, helpdesk etc.
- To provide knowledge-based services and connecting the library users by social interactive media to inform, mentor and train.
- To adjust the media analysis to have well managed information services, for the identification of trends and ability to assess for future decisions.
- Let the library work as knowledge advisors by pooling the user requests and creation of information maps.

iv. Digitization : The trends in digitization suggest following aspects:

- Presence of unique information items.
- Consideration of "just-in-case" factor.
- Inclusion of "just-in-time" reason to initiate access based service.
- Digitizing on as-needed basis if there are research requests by users.

v. Configuring the library space for services : To help the library, and building collection and providing users' desired books, the physical space is recreated by having more electronic documents in the collection, increasing physical space. Thus providing more space to users for interactive learning in a nice ambience has been a need as well as aim. The reconfiguration of library space as well as physical collection depends upon digitization, and weeding out.

vi. Inclusion of Technologies : There is always need of technologies and tools to enhance the library services. To strengthen the library service deliverance, there are couples of technologies which have proven very impressive in case of virtual environment. These technologies include presence of Wi-Fi, well connected numbers of computer systems, e-book readers etc. These technologies are to be exploited and exhausted to provide access to resources as well as content. The well coordinated symbiotic relation between the library and computer center paves way for digital information services.

The use of technology based platforms is supposed to be as below:

- Use of new technology is housekeeping functions to redirect the inside ambience technology oriented and to motivate the library staff for inclusion of the same in services.
- Using the work-life cycle to handle the problems arising at various stages such as assigning the task, any technology related limitation or bringing the outside contribution as support in completing the task.
- Implementing the new components of technologies such as open access and open source into the academic library environment where the prices of commercial publications and software are sky reaching. To use

"Drupal" as web interface of library is one of the examples. At the same time, to find and provide the information tools such as Mediawiki could be used.

HOW TO BUILD A LIBRARY MADE OF EVERLASTING COLLECTION!

The collection building in library depends on the ground realities of the past practices in the acquisition section and the strong acquisition policies. Inclusion of electronic resources has become mandatory and the requirements of the students are fulfilled by the librarians who are the facilitator and responsible to collection building. When a library wants to modernize itself, the collection building along with management of digital content with the licensing becomes must. The key factors to purchase the electronic content are the tech-friendly facilities and 'the experience' a user receives. But the high costs and other issues somehow create cumbersome situations yet the library has to opt for the same to modernize the collection and services. The vision and role of librarian is very crucial in negotiation process leading towards licensing of the e-books and e-journals especially.

THE TORCHBEARERS: POLICY FRAMEWORKS

The policies function as the guiding principles for decision making process and help in avoidance of ambiguous conditions. The proliferation of services and number of staff in a library often create the environment when absence of proper and strong policies may provide a platform for confused decisions. The enforceability is of course by the competent authority but the establishment of various explicit frameworks of guidelines supports the library in creating and providing services. The policies are very much needed due to high use of information technology and security concerns, the privacy matters of library users can also not be ignored.

The areas are such as use of information technology, compliance with licensing and other aspects, dealing with social networking tools, collaboration with other libraries and the virtual environment.

The policies provide framework for the building blocks for an academic library in a way that, the broader the areas covered, the integrity of housekeeping functions and services are held in an efficient manner. The policies provide a coherent framework to relate with parent organization as well as the users to be served. The library progresses with the help of policies that guide to sustain the innovative services within the tight budgets and without being harassed by complex situations. The policies support in building the following assets for the library:

Accumulating Right Relations

The library needs to build relationship with the other supporting sections or departments such as Computer/IT departments; legal cell and administrative branch for the better understanding of complexities arose due to mix of technology and copyright etc. The delicate relationship of various licensing elements with the technological modes of deliverance is almost dependent upon the coordinated expertise of the other functional components in the organization, other than the library.

Also the content delivery requires the preplanned and organized system so that it can be delivered at the time of requirement or it can be arranged. The choice of centralized or decentralized content depends on the types of users' expectations and the infrastructure to be developed. The target audiences for the library services are the people, who belong to the parent organization in which the academic library serves. The content delivery happens searching from the inside in-house or acquired sources as well as the interlibrary loan. The content access and the delivery are very much different for the students and researchers. The library has to design a system to deliver information for both kinds of users.

The ongoing projections are as following:

- Moving from traditional library services to virtual mechanism of services.
- Emphasis on digital content and delivery.
- Use of electronic communication and social media for interaction and interface.
- Provision of targeting the various kinds of users and designing "research-based services", "people-intensive services".
- Increased use of digital platforms as interface and interactive portals and smart phones as the young generation is smart and tech-savvy.
- Strategically shifting towards the staff that interact and analyses rather than sitting to be demanded by the users. The library staff is trained itself to interact to support the library community.
- To identify the areas those require research to develop user-centric services and develop them in different steps.
- To install the security means and measures to instill a safe information environment and maintain the library user privacy.
- Restructuring the library staff, management and services in order to include digital information services as well create room for innovation.
- Increasing digital literacy and licensing education in order to enhance library staff for better negotiations and resources' use.
- Creating a library that is innovative and user friendly in nature.

FUNDAMENTALS AND FRAMEWORKS

To strengthen the existing library services the review of policies and amendments are must to do. There are certain areas which are continuously observed and may ask for timely revision of policies. The areas in general are associated with the efficient functioning, financial aspects and collection building. The following components reflect an in-depth study and action for the improved library services:

i. Circulation and Inter Library Loan Policies

The front desk of library is the Circulation counter and it can be said that the user requests the service from this section most of the time. Since there are myriad kinds of requests, demands and the limitations so the circulation-section as well as Inter Library Loan facility faces various tricky situations. It is difficult to provide answers to all queries but the clear guidelines provide how to do.

ii. IT and Digital Infrastructure

How to develop the library into a modern and functional platform depends on the availability of information technology infrastructure. To lead the library towards digital information and IT based services require policies for continuous development.

iii. Services for Users

The properly framed policies enhance the service environment and pave way for innovative services. The policies provide mechanisms for routine services as well as the services based on Assistive technologies. The library is meant for the user community that can use the library regardless of their physical status.

iv. Policies for Library Liaisons and Collaborations

Academic libraries are meant to collaborate with academic community which involves students, the faculty members. The liaison between library and faculty members augments the library usage by creating awareness, correlating with courses etc. The policies thus formed to identify the method and implementation of liaison services.

v. Policies for Scholarly Communication and Open Access

To enhance the research oriented services and augment the research output of the university, framing of policies is necessary to facilitate the scholarly communication. There have been various programs to inform the users about the open access and other technologies. The open access movement has taken the academic libraries by its stroll and these libraries should create awareness among the library users. To dream about the organization on world research map, the path encompasses better library services and highly informed users.

vi. Policies for Library Users

To discover the library resources and utilize library services, the academic library is supposed to create those guidelines for the users which direct them towards the better collection building, services and preparation for future that takes place every now and then whenever 'technology-push' or the 'user demand' is there. These policies do not move without the guidelines for staff. The library staff is also enrolled in the library development program on the basis of explicit and professionaly guided policies. These policies provide mechanisms to explore the resources and services in a highly competent environment where the librarians have to modify their routines to satisfy the library users.

A PANACHE OF SERVICES IN ACADEMIC LIBRARY

The academic libraries are meant to deliver services for variety of users such as post graduate students, researchers, faculty members and the academic visitors who may hail from any corner of the world with an unspecified kind of information requirements. The dissemination of information has changed to accessibility, and books are no more the properties of thick volumes. In the extremely altered scenario, the role of librarian moves towards the creation of innovative services to meet users' expectation rather than custodian of library. The following prerogatives relate to the information environment:

i. Prioritizing the responsibilities

The definitive strategy is to have kinds of library services but it requires prioritizing at the very moment. The planning of levels of services needs the focus on targets to be achieved. This may include the number of readers' services to IT based infrastructural facilities.

ii. Collection Building and Spacing

The library has reading resources which belong to users; this idea is very much into the mind of an academic librarian. The thorough and extensive documents collection in the form of print books, electronic books, gifted items etc. consume much time in planning about the decision regarding the number of copies, items to be included in the collection, their worth and, of course, the price to build a good collection that comes into forever use, is possible.

iii. Deposit and Access

The collection building and prioritizing brings another chapter in the book of innovative services in the form of in-house development of repositories of research output, archiving the old documents for access and preservation etc. Creating a platform to bring together entire research contribution of researchers, faculty members, is one of its kinds of platforms to build and serve for the users. Setting a digital platform on the basis of open source software and inputting the documents or hyperlinks under the purview of copyright is something to grow.

iv. Strategy Group and Team Building

To continue with the better library services, the innovation is required in the staffing as well as creation of a group or team that constantly watches the problems and works for them. Identification of the leaders within the library staff and making them responsible to look after various areas for the comfort of library users is another priority towards the development of efficient library.

REFERENCES

1. Alan Poulter, (2007) "From the compleat librarian to the InfoLiterate citizen?", Library Review, Vol. 56 Iss: 4, pp.288 - 291
2. Benki S.H. Womboh, (2002) "The predicament of librarianship: its problems and prospects in Nigeria", Library Review, Vol. 51 Iss: 5, pp.256 - 262Claudett Lambert, Nadine Newman, (2012) "Second career librarians: teachers transitioning to librarianship", Library Review, Vol. 61 Iss: 6, pp.428 - 446
3. Dantrea Hampton, Amanda Peach & Benjamin Rawlins. Extending Library Services with QR Codes. The Reference Librarian, Volume 53, Issue 4, October 2012, pages 403-414
4. David McMenemy, (2007) "Reviewing libraries and librarianship: what has changed in 80 years?", Library Review, Vol. 56 Iss: 1, pp.8 - 10
5. Denise Koufogiannakis, Ellen Crumley, (2006) "Research in librarianship: issues to consider", Library Hi Tech, Vol. 24 Iss: 3, pp.324 - 340
6. Emily Love, (2010) "Generation next: recruiting minority students to librarianship", Reference Services Review, Vol. 38 Iss: 3, pp.482 - 492
7. Fakkirappa Kattimani Shivaputrappa , R. Naik Ramesh , (2013) "Evaluation of librarianship and ICT skills of library and information professionals working in the engineering college libraries in Karnataka, India: a survey", Program: electronic library and information systems, Vol. 47 Iss: 4, pp.345 - 369
8. Farzana Shafique, (2007) "Librarianship: how is the future

perceived by librarians in Pakistan?", Library Review, Vol. 56 Iss: 9, pp.811 - 820

9. H. Kumar Percy Jayasuriya & Frances M. Brillantine. Student Services in the 21st Century: Evolution and Innovation in Discovering Student Needs, Teaching Information Literacy, and Designing Library, 2.0-Based Student Services. *Legal Reference Services Quarterly*, Volume 26, Issue 1-2, December 2007, pages 135-170

10. Karsten Nissen Pedersen, (2006) "Librarianship: from collections control to tools understanding", New Library World, Vol. 107 Iss: 11/12, pp.538 - 551

11. Jayati Chaudhuri, (2008) "Journal of Web Librarianship", Online Information Review, Vol. 32 Iss: 2, pp.286 - 287

12. Jeffrey A. Knapp, (2012) "Plugging the "whole": librarians as interdisciplinary facilitators", Library Review, Vol. 61 Iss: 3, pp.199 - 214

13. JNU Library website. http://lib.jnu.ac.in/

14. M.A. Bello, (1992) "The choice of librarianship as a career", New Library World, Vol. 93 Iss: 3

15. M. Madhusudhan, V. Nagabhushanam, (2012) "Web based library services in university libraries in India: an analysis of librarians' perspective", The Electronic Library, Vol. 30 Iss: 5, pp.569 - 588

16. Maitrayee Ghosh, (2007) "ICT and AIDS literacy: a challenge for information professionals in India", Program, Vol. 41 Iss: 2, pp.134 - 147

17. Robert Vaagan, Sigrid Holm, (2004) "Professional values in Norwegian librarianship", New Library World, Vol. 105 Iss: 5/6, pp.213 - 217

18. Shelagh Fisher, (1990) "Team Librarianship: The Case for the Branch Librarian", Library Review, Vol. 39 Iss: 6

19. Stuart James, (2012) "Advances in Librarianship, Volume 33", Library Review, Vol. 61 Iss: 3, pp.231 – 232

20. V.S. Sivankutty, Jinu Sudhakaran, (2011) "The use of online newspapers among librarians in India", Library Hi Tech News, Vol. 28 Iss: 1, pp.10 - 12

21. V.K. Thomas, Chitra Satpathi, J.N. Satpathi, (2010) "Emerging challenges in academic librarianship and role of library associations in professional updating", Library Management, Vol. 31 Iss: 8/9, pp.594 - 609

3

Modernization in Library Scenario

First to Clean and Make It Calm!

About the various actions taken to pave way for modernity in library! Initiating and limiting certain activities/practices/services to create an environment for new practices.

INTRODUCTION

The role of library has changed due to nature of its upbringing and relations towards the users in the modern society. Conversing about the academic library also informs the gradual development in the history of academic arena. From card catalogue to IT based OPACs or cutting-pasting of newspaper items in everyday routine to electronic clipping, everything seems drastically changing in the academic libraries. The momentous change in the library world has always been a centrifugal force for the academic libraries.

The new millennium also witnessed the outsourcing concepts in the academic libraries as well as the digitization run. The shifting paradigms due to information technology and the perceptions of the leadership in the library scenario have created new platforms for the users' engagement with the libraries. The embankment of digital initiatives has created another device for the development of the libraries.

THE BACKGROUND ISSUES

There have been various factors and issues that were relevant to draw the attention to make the library modern but have an explicit examination. These issues are explained as following:

i. Creating platform for student learning

The library transforms itself into a hub for learning by establishing new norms to meet users' academic needs. The programs for information literacy throughout the year have been designed to keep in touch with the changing tastes and targets of readers.

ii. Library Rules and Various Policies

Being a prominent center of higher education, the learning through research is the basic assumption of university. Formulation of library policies, and rules for academic community for day-today activities became must so that any previous policies do not affect the library in a new environment if those policies did not conform to changed expectations of users.

iii. Collaborations and Liaisons

The thorough collaboration and liaison programs are required in order to remain in touch with the ongoing course related activities where library can play an active role in supporting their academic purposes and pursuits. The professional relations with a mission to serve the organizational goals enhance the strong roots for collaborations and liaisons with the other organizations as well as faculty members or students. The contributions from the supporting organizations or individuals are visible in various programs and services of library.

iv. Presence and visibility

The web presence and effective visibility of library is must to create awareness of anything new from the library and augment reach of the student and library vice-versa. This kind of rigorous activity creates a platform for marketing the information services and resources as well. The promotional programs are also informed to users through the web via official website and social media.

v. Relating to community in academic realm

Libraries do not exist to stand as a building and sit in the anticipation of users; yet for the active relations with the community, these serve. No matter it is the academic library, still it has to relate with the users at various levels such as students at post graduate programs or the highly specific community of researchers. The community building with the academic users is almost a result providing exercise in a desired way. Developments of those programs that provide direct access to library are necessary for the learning other than classroom teaching or formal relation with the library.

vi. Avenues for changed methods of Scholarly Communication

Since there have been changes and developments in the ways that were the definite course for scholarly communication, the role of library also broadens. The library is supposed to inform its users about the open access and other non-commercial publishing platforms. There have been various programs for creating awareness of these kinds of avenues for the researchers at JNU. The library should become a mean of transition in each area that it relates to, and find suitable to enhance its role in academic niche.

INCREASING IMPORTANCE OF LIBRARIES IN HIGHER EDUCATION

The strategic plans in higher education institutions include library from the inception, since the library is considered the heart of university. The planning, implementation and thorough care lead the library to serve better in a university environment. The urgency of better university library services also demonstrates the vision of national level academic or education agencies. The broad goals help in designing of a new library as well as improving the current structure. To strengthen and evaluate the competencies of university library needs the leadership and a vision to initiate. Redefining the roles of university library depends on the service model and the preparations to aim the goals. The areas and directions to be attentive are as following:

i. Identification of strong and valuable areas, services and assets

The first and foremost action was to identify those resources and services of JNU library which have been considered the valuable legacy. The news clipping service, languages collections are few of the areas which have been instrumental in making the JNU library specific. Document delivery service has been crucial in establishing the relation with other libraries to have resource sharing.

ii. Restructuring the library spaces

The JNU library was established way back into last millennium during nineteen sixties. The number of users, kinds of collections and services were according to requirements of that time. The changed scenario in context of collections and services during current times demanded some shuffle and rearrangements. Changes into physical spaces by shifting collections to the areas where more visibility is available for enhanced usage have been done.

Identification of areas which can be helpful for augmented movements of readers kept open. Shifting the bound periodicals or science collection to provide more sitting facility is something that was carefully done.

iii. Converting professional capacities into leadership

It is significant to provide a platform to the library staff in increased capacity to participate in decision making by identifying the problems. The library staff is trained to let the services carried on efficiently yet their direct involvement gives an opportunity to inform more about the students' problems or expectations. Such information helps in designing new services or improving the current ones.

iv. Enhancing the expertise and growth

To sustain the development and modernity in the JNU library it was considered essential to have continuous and rigorous training of staff at each level. The senior level staff is responsible for leadership and problem-solving whereas the staffs at mid level and lower level have learnt the tactics of better interaction and gesture to provide services with professional commitment. The development of various platforms such as library website and increased use of library software compel an indirect training as well as communicative feature.

The identification of key areas supports the library to move in a streamlined manner. To avoid overlapping in planning the testing at initial phases with the right proportions of clusters of checkpoints is necessary. For every activity there could not be a 'pilot project' yet the strategies propel the right directions. Such path breaking actions in the JNU library leveraged the professional competencies and expertise. Various areas such as users' preferences in context with print or digital sources, commercial platforms or open access, self services or assisted services etc. have been challenging but provided the library to learn new lessons and emerge as a library with difference.

The exposure to multimedia, modern communicating devices and various types of resource platforms have been the boons and bane, both in disguise for the JNU library. The students desire and expect the same experience which is found in other libraries or heard from their friends. Whereas Google functions the one and only major interface for the information search yet the library had been in search of such facility for its students and faculty members. Though there has been a strong OPAC and other windows to peep inside the library collection but the ease and single search window was very much in demand. To convert university library from "hardly get used" to the ultimate source of academic pursuit was a challenge for the library leadership. The value added services get total appreciation when the users are able to find the library resources at one click. To compete with major search engines and answering to users' needs were the cause to have a 'discovery' like service at JNU library.

UNDERSTANDING THE NATURE OF LIBRARY SERVICES

To have gateways for the users those let them enter into the vast reservoir of information, it has been crucial to understand the ongoing developments and changes into the university academic environment. While deciding to have a separate library website and group of specific services; the users' expectations, current technologies and enhancing infrastructure are taken into consideration. There are following two major facets of modernization included in strategies and action:

i. Customer services and experiences

The academic users such as students, researchers and

faculty members are the esteemed customers of university libraries. Though the library concentrates on the users' expectations and tries to provide the information products and services which are most useful and widely accessed by them yet the library has to find out the means and methods which define and explain the right choice and demands from the users' side. The degree of expectation depends on the library's exercise on understanding the customers' needs. The web based services may support the library in giving a gateway yet the continuous update on other ways is always there on the side of library. The time to time feedbacks and anticipated services helps the library.

ii. Facilitating wide access and augmenting the richness

To facilitate access is directly concerned with the awareness and retrieval. Understanding users' requests, entailing the each possible action to create access and facilitate the information retrieval supports the vision of library. The concept of "e-services" to the users is very much an indispensible entity in the service arena of academic library. Since services are the basic means to relate to users, examination of library services in comparison with World Wide Web features and facilities becomes must because the users want the library to function at their fingertips as easy as the web-based information. Incorporation of UGC guidance in universities enforces the JNU library too, to have high quality resources and outcomes form the university. To include modern services the path encompasses web-based library services such as presence of OPAC, web portal, direct links to e-resources, single search platforms; and modern mobile gadget based information services such as downloading e-books to read later, accessing internet etc. There is tremendous growth in network based library services such as having electronic theses on intranet, institutional repository and facilitating the information services with utmost privacy of the users. There needs to be emphasis on 'personal learning networks' in order to augment the method of discussion as a popular mean to connect with fellow researchers and students at JNU.

The integral designing of library is more significant instead of having few services for quite some time. The availability of resources and services along with the pleasant library staff comprises above noted both the facets. The service experience of the library users has been one of the hidden elements of designing a new platform with in the library. There are two aspects which go on side by side; users' expectations and the quality based library services. The satisfaction of the users turns into profits of the library as there is no other mean to calculate. The following components create value based services in academic library in context with a customer oriented approach:

i. Identification of constraints and resources

ii. Delivery mechanisms

iii. Usage studies

iv. Active partnership

v. Maintenance of reader relationship.

In fact the library's relationship with the customers is a tedious process involving mutual expressions and understanding leading towards the generation of facilities such as direct requests from students about the required books and programs of learning such as JNU forum for Mutual Learning. The strong relationship between the library users and library informs about the developments the JNU library have made during last 3-4 years. Such relations directly help in collection building and creation of services that are widely used at JNU library. Certainly a library is overburdened sometimes in order to satisfy the users' needs, which are varied in nature and always urgent in queue. The measurement of user satisfaction depends on the fare and feedback library is having with the users. To provide quality based service library has taken into consideration of keeping exceptionally trained library staff at the interactive zones as well as outsourcing of skilled people. No matter what the situation is, the goal is users' satisfaction. Creation of interactive library website or having helpdesk are few of the examples along with solving the acquisition related problems when users confront with trained staff in the concerned section.

Abilities such as documentation; and job competencies as planning in advance or organizing the resources based on personal relations reflect the commitment of library staff. Providing immediate response to readers is one of the time bound services though not a formal one. The staff being conductive and courteous is necessary in the current scenario of academic libraries. The knowledge of working as well as keeping the customers' needs in mind masters the library staff. Utilization of competencies and technological expertise is must and that has been properly learnt by the staff by embracing the day-today routine needs of users. The service with attitude is not the motto yet the preparation of information products with highly demanded information services is the welcoming on the part of users as well. There are no "traditional assumptions" but the modern approaches exist. With few thanks and large number of complaints create a picture of constant improvement and the room for more in the library.

CREATING A QUALITY IMAGE OF LIBRARY

Carrying a legacy of having different and rare collections not only in the country but also in the continent is worth to be proud but the improvement in image of library in the world that is highly dominated by information technology needs overhauling in its structure as well as the perception among the users and other librarians. The much needed quality image creation has been possible due to proper policies to achieve library goals and enforceable mechanisms for implementation. Without a framework the library could not put itself into right direction of action. It has been leading towards a better "quality image" by the virtue of right collections and services.

The management practices in the library should conform to JNU policies and the goals tend to guide the formal acts of the central library. The quality image has been achieved by establishing the individual standards on the basis of targeted duties to the library staff. Without quality work there could not have materialize the achievements of JNU library. Surely there have been many learning lessons to have reached up to this stage. Keeping the library users' needs in the goals of library services has been an effective instrument to create an image of serving library which is the ultimate dream of every library worker. It is the user perception that defines and designs the image of library all-around. Interpretation of information needs, and provisions to meet them articulate the values created by the library and certainly its image.

THE NEW PARADIGMS AND VISTA

The library plans to embark its service journey towards web-based as well as well managed conventional services. Definitely the library needs to create the awareness about the web based library's preparation and services. There is need to increase the access of library web site to access online databases. The purposes to access may range from accessing/ downloading the full text articles to online tutorials. The extended services are concerned with the following:

i. The student may need the information to complete their class and research assignments.

ii. The researchers find the information related for their research purposes.

iii. Increased value of information sources will state the use of digital reference service.

iv. The library will provide strong and very informative FAQs so that the website reader is getting answers without coming to library.

v. There should be provisions for online feedback from the library users and visitors.

vi. The extension needs including providing the alert services and tutorials for how to access to digitized materials.

Moving from traditional mode of library services there is need to emphasize the face to face services to deliver the appropriate response and in the online environment, services are carefully designed to assist users using the technology such as communication via email and social media. The comfort with the technology plays a great role and the young library users are very much enthusiastic as well as well–versed to use the digital services. These aspects are useful in designing and using the online reference service while using e-mail activity or the help of web forms. Online services are more sophisticated because there is no "human face". It may also take more time to develop trust and win the confidence of library users. Modernization of library is not without having trust of users where the users are seeking convenience in expressing their information requirements.

Access to library staffs that directly are responsible for digital services is must for library users. The library staff functions as a bridge to support the users as well as modern and newly introduced services. The proliferation of information demands modernization as well as in house homework for the academic libraries before appearance. The well trained staff in order to serve the users in problems such as login-password, guest user facilities or who can access what kind of resources are dealt by the staff. The library staff functions as a quick guide for the users. In a very informal way, the library staff helps users in developing online information search skills. The tutorials with subject specific search help novice readers. Repackaging the information services is based on ground-breaking changes in the library environment and mindsets. The entire service experience for the users depends on the preparation and provisions for the future library services. The long lasting effects of initial labors by the library are seen when the users turn back to library.

TAMING THE INTEGRITY

The library has begun its journey towards maintaining few commitments with itself such as:

i. Cultural shift towards a client oriented services
ii. Inculcating skills in library management
iii. Nurturing the healthy environment
iv. Marketing as well as feedback
v. Providing a reliable library platform

It is significant to develop an environment which is user-friendly as well as staff-nurturing. When the library provides a platform to users to share their views as well as complaints, leads towards better interaction, lesser known areas of concern and where to improve. The staff is also told to respond about the users' problems and suggestions so that a level of trust can be created. The users' suggestions, demands may prove very helpful in creating interfaces, generating of alerting services etc. The kind of organization and restructuring library needs also depend on close communication with the users. To create a 'Brand Library' and to popularize it, the necessary aspects are challenges that are faced by the library staff day by day. The active partnership that library should have with its users is based on the recognition of deliverance of excellent services. The library planned to have satisfied library users as they will inform others about better library services.

NEW DESIGNS AND PATTERNS IN LIBRARY SERVICES

The library chose to bring out few changes in patterns of library services and interfaces to refresh the look and feel. The current technologies, in fact the recent trends, have been highly motivating to initiate the alteration work in the existing service structure as well as the library visibility. Having presence in social media by creating a page of JNU Library or the library staff on social media informing and interacting with fellow librarians and library users has been a small step. Having a dedicated news section on library portal reflects the close connection with what is happening around. The students as well as people from outside the JNU are informed about the campus activities.

Informing the users about the specific events such as workshops meant for them or the events related with "JNU Mutual Forum for Learning" are other methods to be in touch with the library customers and having fresh visual of various library events, especially concerned with library users. The facilities such as Site Search, or featured books, new arrivals are must for literary quests. The query starts why the new beginnings require a fresh platform! When the library embarks on a journey of highly sophisticated technology based pathway, certainly there are areas that demand urgent attention from the library leadership.

Presenting a library with the information about it and the services desired by the users is really an uphill task. The information include about the library resources and how to access within the set criteria of meaningful use. The services may range from demanding latest information to solutions for past papers too. The library designed itself keeping the following aspects:

i. Update information about A-Z of library and resources.

ii. Providing quick links to resources

iii. Categorization of information and services for the types of users related with library.

Why the library needed a change and a direction to move on!

The digital age has compelled the big businesses to change and comply with the commands of technologies and so is the library. The users are the guide to library and their demands and expectations are the motivators for an academic library. The way World Wide Web and Internet affected the methods to find and access information has been enforcing the academic libraries to change. The library has been trying to shift from a conventional framework to a digital-savvy structure which is modular in nature and accustomed to changing environment. The methods of lending books and finding reference service have been highly changed scenarios in libraries. There are reasons for this dramatic shift in the library development such as:

- To provide the interface to ask in online platform.
- To introduce mobile-based applications and facilities to access information.
- To identify the new gadgets and devices put into use for library.
- Use of technology to organize print resources and management.
- Having RFID or any other identification based system to ease the library mechanism.
- Customization of methods so that library users can recommend books/documents of their need without much hassle.

The involvement of library users is increasing and it is necessary to understand the changed scenario. To include the collaboration of library and faculty in the users' services, the priorities have been as below:

i. To have coordination with the learning centers.

ii. To organize the learning sessions in order to inform how the library can play a great role in enhancing learning.

iii. To create a niche of comprehensive learning.

iv. Engaging the users in collection development in library. To have a definite plan to execute and increase popularity of steps taken by library, there has been constant improvement in the handling of various policies and practices.

The factors responsible for cleaning up and creating the segments in three dimensional frame of strategy, actions and services are as following:

i. Ongoing developments and changes in using library

Using library through online interfaces, gateways etc.

ii. Changes in the way users perceive an academic library

It is beyond the printed bibliography to having sessions on reference management tools and plagiarism check.

iii. Greater online information sources and access

Except going to library, the remote access goes well and the round of clock availability of online resources. The exploration of library services enhances the platform of JNU library in being a prominent library in north India. The transition of library certainly opened new vistas yet much more to imbibe in the library environment to address the right kind of services to users with right kinds of resources. There are margins to be defined as well as to be broken so that the library expands its limits towards the unachieved.

iv. Inclusion of more technology with less hassle

The gadgets and competition to use most modern equipments have landed the users in a zone that library may exploit in its favor, in order to reach more number of users by providing access to library beyond the walls.

v. Informing the users about the library

Quite significant it is for the users to know about their library and what it does for them! It is more interesting to identify how the library can be more useful for the users. It is always important for the library to devote towards defined mechanisms of building collections as per requirements of users. Sometimes there is variation in their choices yet the patterns in demand are the chief source for designing services or acquiring new documents. Over a certain period of time the information sources lose value so there should be some checkpoint in determining the demand or choice to be 'right' and always 'useful' for others if studying in same area.

Meeting the demands and finding those requested titles useful for the future hold the key to building sound collection in particular subject area or research. The library can have a choice to offer more e-books if readers want.

i. *Freeing the staff by automating routine jobs:* Library automation and implementation of identification techniques support the library staff in saving time to utilize in other services as well offering the users to complete tasks where the library staff is not needed. Such aspects bring more knowledge to users while doing library activities themselves such depositing the books or submitting the fines. To have a library kiosk to check out books is one of the simple examples.

ii. *Technology before the pace!:* What if the gadgets are preloaded with supporting software or library offers to install or download apps to read e-books. Since the library plans to move towards more digital collection, such activities will clearly support the library-user relations as well enhance the usage of collections. The 'Cyber Library' is one of its kinds of initiatives towards users' services.

Teaching the students about downloading e-books and additional software have been routine activities yet strengthening processes at JNU library.

THE GUIDING PRINCIPLES IN LIBRARY

The academic libraries also need guiding principles just as the students or researchers. These principles are mentoring fellow to not to deviate and offer information and services. The libraries offer knowledge and services yet a gap of changing conditions and harsh developments are the problematic areas where the libraries need speculations and introspections. These observations definitely may serve as guiding force in order to decide the types of developments to be made and define the limit of extent to which the library needs to march. The survival and significance of academic library is entirely dependent on how the strategies are made and implemented in the academic community. The community to be served is always demanding so the continuous planning and policy making by the library along with avoiding any biasness as facilitators. A flexible approach and embracing new technologies help in chasing the horizons that can become the real platforms based on competencies.

The crossroads before an academic library are always cumbersome yet require kinds of opportunities to move up to the global standards and meet the users' expectations. The pressures to afford everything to serve the readers also compel and motivate the academic library. The problem of identity crisis does not appear before the library but there is long way of concerns to keep up with the momentum. The digital natives or modern users in library are the partners in promotion of library and its collections, services. By applying certain methods and mechanisms, the library can be before the faces of its users and on their learning radar. The focus on user experience frames a guiding principle for an adept academic library.

THE BUMPY ROAD AND RIDING!

Certain issues are before the library such as how to imbibe ideal librarianship among the library staff, how to direct the library services towards innovation. Indulging more in the technology by way of automation and digital library services also cost time and planning. Reducing the involvement of old patterns and practices as obstacles is highly required. The reluctance to initiate or any apprehension on the part of library staff is repercussions for the development. The struggling library towards potential innovation brings itself at the door of new dawn. The library neither needs to push the technology nor put the traditions on the brink of losing legacy due to forces of current information technologies; the concerns are bigger and closer too.

REFERENCES

1. Abdul Mannan Khan, (2010) "Managing collection development and organization in globalizing Indian university libraries", Collection Building, Vol. 29 Iss: 1, pp.15 - 21
2. Anilkumar Hanumappa , Mallikarjun Dora , Viral Navik , (2014) "Open Source Software solutions in Indian libraries", Library Hi Tech, Vol. 32 Iss: 3, pp.409 - 422
3. B.T. Sampath Kumar, B.S. Biradar, (2010) "Use of ICT in college libraries in Karnataka, India: a survey", Program, Vol. 44 Iss: 3, pp.271 - 282
4. Bruce E. Massis , (2014) "Library marketing: moving between traditional and digital strategies", New Library World, Vol. 115 Iss: 7/8, pp.405 - 408
5. David Bradbury, (1993) "British Library Document Supply Centre Strategy: THE NEXT TEN YEARS", Interlending & Document Supply, Vol. 21 Iss: 3, pp.7 - 11

6. Dillip K. Swain, K.C. Panda, (2009) "Use of electronic resources in business school libraries of an Indian state: A study of librarians' opinion", The Electronic Library, Vol. 27 Iss: 1, pp.74 - 85

7. Graham Matthews , Graham Walton , (2014) "Strategic development of university library space: Widening the influence", New Library World, Vol. 115 Iss: 5/6, pp.237 - 249

8. Guo Jing, Chen Jin, (2009) "The innovative university library: strategic choice, construction practices and development ideas", Library Management, Vol. 30 Iss: 4/5, pp.295 - 308

9. Ina Fourie, (2012) "Collaboration and personal information management (PIM)", Library Hi Tech, Vol. 30 Iss: 1, pp.186 - 193

10. Ivana Hebrang Grgic, (2011) "Gifts in Croatian public and academic libraries", Collection Building, Vol. 30 Iss: 4, pp.167 - 171

11. Jeanne M. Brown, Jennifer L. Fabbi, Cheryl Taranto, (2005) "Branch libraries and technology: impact of a new main library", Library Hi Tech, Vol. 23 Iss: 1, pp.90 - 101

12. Jennifer Rowley, (2011) "Should your library have an innovation strategy?", Library Management, Vol. 32 Iss: 4/5, pp.251 - 265

13. Jerry Henzel, Barbara S. Hutchinson, Anne Thwaits, (2006) "Using web services to promote library extension collaboration", Library Hi Tech, Vol. 24 Iss: 1, pp.126 – 141

14. Joseph J. Branin, (1989) "Information Policies for Collection Development Librarians", Collection Building, Vol. 9 Iss: 3/4, pp.19 - 23

15. Juha Kettunen, (2007) "The strategic evaluation of academic libraries", Library Hi Tech, Vol. 25 Iss: 3, pp.409 - 421

16. Kelly Riddle , (2015) "Creating policies for library publishing in an institutional repository: Exploring purpose, scope, and the library's role", OCLC Systems & Services: International digital library perspectives, Vol. 31 Iss: 2, pp.59 - 68

17. Leo Favret, (2000) "Benchmarking, annual library plans and best value: the implications for public libraries", Library Management, Vol. 21 Iss: 7, pp.340 - 348

18. Lynne Brindley, (2006) "Re defining the library", Library Hi Tech, Vol. 24 Iss: 4, pp.484 - 495

19. Maitrayee Ghosh, Ipsheet Ghosh, (2009) "ICT and information strategies for a knowledge economy: the Indian experience", Program, Vol. 43 Iss: 2, pp.187 - 201

20. Maitrayee Ghosh, S.C. Biswas, V.K.J. Jeevan, (2006) "Strategic

cooperation and consortia building for Indian libraries: models and methods", Library Review, Vol. 55 Iss: 9, pp.608 - 620

21. Maria Luisa Calanag, Koichi Tabata, Shigeo Sugimoto, (2004) "Linking preservation metadata and collection management policies", Collection Building, Vol. 23 Iss: 2, pp.56 - 63
22. Michael A. Germano, Shirley M. Stretch Stephenson, (2012) "Strategic value planning for libraries", The Bottom Line, Vol. 25 Iss: 2, pp.71 - 88
23. P.K. Sudarsan, (2006) "A resource allocation model for university libraries in India", The Bottom Line, Vol. 19 Iss: 3, pp.103 - 110
24. Roy J. Adams, (1995) "Strategic information systems and libraries", Library Management, Vol. 16 Iss: 1, pp.11 - 17
25. Siriginidi Subba Rao, (1998) "CD publishing and its scenario in India", New Library World, Vol. 99 Iss: 3, pp.118 – 124
26. Sneha Tripathi, Aditya Tripathi, (2010) "Privacy in libraries: the perspective from India", Library Review, Vol. 59 Iss: 8, pp.615 - 623
27. Veerbala Sharma, Dinesh K. Gupta, (2012) "Outsourcing of human resources in science and technology libraries of northern India", The Bottom Line, Vol. 25 Iss: 4, pp.163 - 176
28. Samuel Olu Adeyoyin, (2005) "Strategic planning for marketing library services", Library Management, Vol. 26 Iss: 8/9, pp.494 - 507
29. Sanjica Faletar Tanackoviæ, Boris Badurina, (2008) "Collaboration as a wave of future: exploring experiences from Croatian archives", Library Hi Tech, Vol. 26 Iss: 4, pp.557 – 574
30. Zhixian Yi, (2008) "Knowledge management for library strategic planning: Perceptions of applications and benefits", Library Management, Vol. 29 Iss: 3, pp.229 - 240
31. Wendy P. Lougee, (1998) "The University of Michigan Digital Library Program: A Retrospective on Collaboration within the Academy", Library Hi Tech, Vol. 16 Iss: 1, pp.51 – 59.

4
Library Designing and Implementing

Not so easy as to fit a new product in an old fashioned framework. Various areas of concern before initiating, facets of library and university policies, rules, orders etc., taken into consideration.

INTRODUCTION

The environment of present organization as well as its impact on library matters for the designing and implementation of a new kind of environment and creating niche for a modernized library services. What we discern at university library, a system of various small libraries in the form of departmental libraries and also various sections in the main library. There are the concepts of branch as well as school libraries within an organization serving the users belonging to a particular area of study and discipline. The functions may be categorized as research oriented services, managing collections for post graduate students or any other kinds as the organization may ask for the benefits of academic community. Certainly the quality and strength of collection along with the satisfactory services are the backbone of academic library keeping in view the objectives, policies and other guiding forces for the library. The designing and implementation of a new library within an existing library needs the coverage of entire spectrum of organization as well as the capacities and preparation of library at any point of observation. The emphasis is placed on the following areas in JNU:

i. Research and research scholars
ii. Post graduate and under-graduate students
iii. Focus on comprehensive collection development
iv. Academic Community building

The facets of library services roam and revolve around the collection development including introductory information sources, advanced kind of information resources for research researchers. The library collection building involves the faculty members also as the reader as well as suggesting to what should be included in the collection. The emphasis is on creating a library environment to make the students "self-sufficient" reader. This creation of self-sufficient reader also depends on organizational policies and how the library implements those policies in order to sustain, and it also creates a modern library in itself. To achieve a desired level of services from library and vice-versa, the organizational support and cooperation is required. Thus leading to have organizational structure well understood and implemented the defined rules; by the library. The space that library needs and the pillars too certainly, are provided by the parent organization in the form of statues, acts, policies, regulations and orders issued time to time. Effective library services are the committed aims of JNU library. The parity with other good libraries and comparable state of services are few areas that draw attention.

THE USERS BEFORE THE LIBRARY'S VISIONS

The library decides any of its goals keeping in mind following types of users:

i. Undergraduate students
ii. Post graduate students
iii. Researchers and
iv. Faculty members

The first and foremost attention seeking users' type is the undergraduate students. Following characteristics associated with them play a great role in understanding the nature and types of collection and services to be designed for them:

i. Least information skills if not nurtured during/in school level studies, so the library gives rigorous library education /orientation to the undergraduate students.
ii. Formal as well as informal kinds of support environment for the undergraduate students.
iii. Usually the undergraduate students have a large share among user population yet at JNU this is the opposite.

The students registered in post graduate courses are sharing a sizeable proportion and number in the users' population so the library has to consider this aspect with well observation and precaution. The instruction and orientation programs for this type of user population demands much attention as they have already learnt the "how to use library" but there is immense emphasis on knowing if their study time can be utilized for the research goals or other competitive examinations. The requirements of this user group are entirely different from the undergraduate students yet the aspirations for research and other goals preoccupy their minds enough to create challenges for the library.

The Researchers

Definitely the researchers' community seems to be task-oriented library users who always come with specific, urgent and sophisticated kind of demand before the library staff. The reasons are hidden in the following factors:

i. Specific area of study
ii. May or may not be fixed schedule for the study
iii. Limited time period in hand to complete their research
iv. Preparation for jobs also

The library always kept the user community in mind; while providing basic services or creating new ones due to their demands and expectations. The research oriented collection and web-based information services are two broad areas that reflect the commitment from the library. The research support system by the library is one fine example. Apart from the learners, the teachers in various capacities such as teaching assistants, senior faculty members etc. are also prominent users of the library. Their information requirements are related to following aspects:

i. Preparations of lectures
ii. Supporting the research at university
iii. Contributing in the existing knowledge world

The library knows its responsibility as a gateway to the knowledge universe and it has been transformed into the serving section of university.

THE REASONS FOR NEW DESIGNING: PROBABILITIES AND CERTAINTIES

The university library has kinds of users, services and relationships with all these facets. The community it serves is the peers as well as pressures if the library plans to reinvent itself and mirrors some ideological workforce. The following components rely on proper planning which is the outcome of well-framed policies and their implementation. The facets may be interrelated as well as interdependent as discussed:

i. The library budget
ii. The library staffing and their qualifications
iii. The physical infrastructure

These components give an eye-opening initial phase for any library to consider their availability and existence. Whereas the library budget is decided and granted is the question of organizational planning. The previous years' expenditures and utilizations in the library are also brought into picture while increasing or decreasing the library budget. The number of persons in library staff are defined at the time of establishment of university may differ later on as the time moves, the requirements guide to increase that number up to the sanctioned strength of staff from the government and other agencies. The physical infrastructure is must for basic services as well as facilitating the future requirements. Various types of users may need different kinds of basic facilities from the library; so the library keeps in planning about the study and research needs for efficient learning environment. There are learning programs by the library that also reflect the need of physical as well as academic infrastructure. While comparing the times back when there was the initial advent of computer systems into Indian universities during the recent few years, the outlook is amazingly different. The library has discerned this change and tried to put the ICT on the map of library and its services. The increased value of user-interaction and the role in collection development has also been as cause and concern for the outcome of present day JNU library. The curriculum of various courses, information and research needs along with the expected services are few measures to improve the library in terms of collection, services.

i. The designing and reinventing is required when the gone era of golden establishment is compared with the fresh ICT imbibed academic scenarios. Borrowing/ Reserve/Reference transactions (face-to-face and virtual)
ii. The recruitment of staff at various times
iii. The contribution of library in the academic goals of JNU

The library becomes proud of its inventions in terms of:

i. Number as well as the diversity of the topics covered in outreach programs
ii. Searches/downloaded digital information sources
iii. Readership/membership and the visitors of the library
iv. Number of computer systems for cyber learning as well as donated to the visually impaired students
v. Growing number of online as well as print resources, strengthening of reader-library interaction for the collection building
vi. The role of central library in academic community building at the campus

LIBRARY PLANNING AND EVALUATION

The goal and vision of library serve as tools to guide the planning and provide a path for projected outcomes. Establishing various divisions in library to renovating the spaces, all actions are related with reinvention of library. The provision of sufficient and trained staff increases the compatibility of library goals with the organizational goals. The designing and building of programs is responsible to showcase the planning process in the form of outcomes. The active mechanism and focus on improvement of library practices identified in order to meet the goals and users' expectations. The proficiencies become the significant tools for performance measurement in context with the deliverance in terms of services to the users. The increased dependence on online resources, services, add further responsibilities such as training to staff and information literacy among the users, inclusive of cost-effective supports in comprehensive methods for the entire library. The users' experiences with library and conduction of information services over a time-period motivate and conduct following assessment activities:

i. Understanding the library's service in context with library staff
ii. Up to the extent incorporation of mission into goals
iii. Continuous development of programs for academic community
iv. Identification of approaches for improvements

PROVISIONS IN UNIVERSITY ACTS AND STATUTES

The organizational laws in the form of University Acts and Statutes provide a base for the various posts and their responsibilities, the library is also well supplied with such provisions. For example, according to section 10 (1), it is given that:

The following shall also be the officers of the University namely: -

i. Dean of Students,
ii. Chief Proctor,
iii. Librarian
iv. Controller of Examinations

Whereas the footnotes declare about the appointment etc. of such officers, for the librarian, given:

(4) (a) The Librarian shall be appointed by the Executive Council and shall be a Whole-time salaried officer of the University.

(b) The duties and powers of the Librarian shall be regulated by the Ordinances

The above mentioned provisions in the Acts and Statues frame the appointment of librarian in university as well as the duties and powers vested in the post.

For the appointment of librarian, the section 27(1) states about the provision of Selection Committees for making recommendations to the Executive Council for appointment to the post of Librarian. Provisions in section

'H' are also related with selection and appointment of librarian.

According to section 11(1), the Court of University is consisted of various Ex-Officio members including the University Librarian. Such provisions reflect various responsibilities and roles of university librarian in view of library's role and contribution in the overall development and growth of university.

According to Section 15 (1), the Academic Council shall consist of the various members including Librarian, whereas the section (16) (i) subject to the provisions of the Act and these Statutes, the Academic Council shall, in addition to all other powers vested in it, have the powers, duties and functions, concerned with 'Libraries and Museums'. In the light of various provisions created in University Acts and Statutes, and other academic objectives, the position of librarian is very significant.

THE CONTEXT OF LIBRARY SERVICES

To design quality library services for various kinds of users is not something to design in a period of overnight. The purposes are purely academic and research oriented; and these services are related with variety of information resources. There are various kinds of services to support academic and research programs such as:

i. Library education and orientation services

ii. Information Skills enhancing services

iii. Innovative Informative programs

iv. Information services based on personal contact, interaction through digital interfaces

v. Library and its services as laboratory to the students for learning

The newly designed services present an improved version of changed library. There are certain factors concerned with users that not only affect but also support in shaping such services. The facets related with innovative and modern library services are another set of few entities which are proven significant such as:

i. Identification of information; anticipated and demanded
ii. Creating knowledge of maximum use of information resources; maximum as well as ethical
iii. Assistance by library staff to the users
iv. Visualizing the future needs, preparations and provisions

These designs and patterns of library development thoroughly relate to teaching and research as the consumers of information are involved in the various processes by their suggestions, interactions etc. This serves as a new angle in the relationship of library and its users and it functions as a step to augment the marketing strategies. The direct relations of library services and users can be understood in the perspectives of following aspects:

i. Offered services and information needs
ii. The feedback collected from users in terms of quality and quantity
iii. Acceptable ratio of library staff and number of library users
iv. Requirement of additional services and interaction with library users

Few questions also support better planning which are stated as following:

v. Are new services, which are needed by users, anticipated and implemented?
vi. Are there any services that have become obsolete and could be eliminated?

TARGETS, CONSIDERATIONS AND INTRINSIC COMPONENTS

The alterations and modernity are closely associated if implemented in a conventional set up of library service. The concentration of resources should be proportional to the users' ability to use library resources sincerely and effectively. The services may be offered on the basis of current resources as well as projected aims of library but the networking with the students and faculty members can also be fruitful in understanding and informing about these services. The requirements are diverse and information sources have the capacity to provide a cohesive approach towards provision of information due to following kinds of needs:

i. Academic needs and interdisciplinary subjects needs

ii. Knowledge of research skills

iii. Information literacy based information support by library staff

iv. Point-of-use aids and awareness among users

The library knows the status of user in terms of library objectives. The library user is ultimate consideration at the goal of library services. The library is dedicated to provide efficient services to meet the users' needs. The library takes an approach which is the combined effort of flexible planning, expertise and innovative vision. The inclusion of supportive staff in these approaches engages the academic user community in various ways which increase opportunities and access. The enthusiasms are fundamentals to interests of library as well as users too, once the services are offered in a desired fashion.

The vision of university library to build an 'organism' capable to serve in global perspectives in the knowledge world has become the sole idea of creation of modern niche. How the library resources and services can become more supportive, the process depends on the utilization of resources and implementation of technologies. The institutional objectives and internationalization of academic pursuits along with the expectations from library have paved way for renovating the information environment. The university's academic strategies are comprised of learning programs, research and a good library that supports these strategies. This type of support comes when the library creates an information environment which is composed of physical as well as virtual information resources supported by ICT based information services. The commitment of library to support and facilitate the range of services with access to myriad information sources requires continuous efforts from library. The constructive role played by library helps in developing independent learning among the students by way of various information services. The library's role in research areas depends on understanding of the following facets:

i. Significance of research
ii. Role of library in understanding information needs
iii. Need of data storage and management
iv. Creation of repository systems
v. Creating awareness among the researchers to utilize Open Access System
vi. Close collaboration of faculty and library
vii. Developing and creating policies on university level for better information access
viii. Partnership of library with students to assist international students

FOCUS ON ENHANCING ACADEMIC PRESTIGE OF UNIVERSITY

Apart from the development of strategies and growth in partnership with various facets of university system, the library has to contribute in building the prestige and reputation of parent organization. There are areas where library has found the correlation with organizational planning such as:

i. Current courses and the introduction of new academic programs.
ii. The benchmarking and diversity in academic excellence.
iii. Various post graduate courses and role of library
iv. Partnership of library with the research activities at JNU campus

The organizational goals help in identification of immediate aims and long term goals. These aims and goals support the need of wide and varied nature of library participation with the academic community. Such participation also reflects the commitment of library towards enhancement of information services. With the example of Assistive technologies for the visually challenged students, the library has shown one of its responsibilities. The role about the skill development and enhancement is well played by the JNU Central Library. As the university does not end the relationship with the alumni community, the library also facilitates them to access the library resources, thus the lifelong relations with the academic community are made and cherished. In creating and maintaining the strong relations based on efficient services, the ICT implementation, digital library, and provisions of remote access to information have been great and instrumental.

Since there are dramatic changes due to social and technological developments, the "JNU environment" is not untouched; the library identified the areas that were potential in nature to nurture the growth and development. The potential areas were grasping the needs of faculty members as well as researchers. A strong example of the same is creating "research support system" for the researchers. The university and library, both are committed towards creation of great research and preservation too, along with the instant access. During these phases, the role of external factors such as admissions of students, academic policies (by Academic Council) and the UGC guidelines for courses/degrees have also supervised and shaped the library roles.

Preserving the electronic theses in order to widen the research access as well check on plagiarism has been an area where the library has marketed itself. The rapid developments in guiding the research arena in the country have also been responsible for increasing role of library. From creating awareness of plagiarism tools to enthuse the originality of research have included many other facets in the range. The developments due to variety in pedagogical method, creation of learning spaces are both supported by library by providing electronic books, journals as well as specific databases. The organization of author workshops and "how to avoid plagiarism awareness" workshops have been very supportive to learners at the university.

KEEPING THE OBJECTIVES AND LIBRARY USERS IN THE PERSPECTIVE

While establishing and improving the university library, certain components are well arranged. The deliverance and creation of learning environment are possible due to following considerations:

i. The value of library user

ii. The dedication of library staff

iii. Ensuring flexibility and avoiding the overlapping of strategies

iv. Learning environment for the library staff due to continuously changing ICT applications

v. Consideration as component of academic community

vi. Promotion of the resources and enhancing accessibility

The context and connect are two very significant aspect of library services, hence with the planning. The context is concerned with the courses and degrees of learning in the university while the connection is established with the users by promoting the information sources and services. The accessibility and prioritizing the services are also associated with this library connection. The conversion of resources into a digital campus was an idea behind the digital library and remote access at JNU campus. The vitality comes when the students are enthusiastic to enter with the break of dawn and do not wish to let it close till the next break of dawn. The 24/7 library is a dream come true for the library readers at JNU. The context once again comes into picture when the image of researcher appears onto the surface of strategies and innovation in the library services. Having the benefits of accessing Open Access resources along with the highly paid e-resources is an appropriate window to find out the research supporting information. Where there is a challenge of having large-scale data management, the Open access movement in country has made university responsive in preparing the institutional repository as well as the submission in "ShodhGanga", an initiative of INFLIBNET. The views and guidelines of funding agencies are also kept in mind while planning for the preparation and provisions for Open Access. Each of the exercise of library is planned to result in increased access and enhance the academic pursuits.

The context is both inward and outward to guide library services. The growth issues are concerned with various programs of universities including the international students at the campus. Various exchange programs of educational contexts are very popular in various schools of university, where the library finds another outlet of serving as well as showcasing the services to the academic users from global background. The means and methods of student intake in the university also compel the library to include the services which are basic as well as advanced in nature. Students from rural background and urban exposures are component of user community. Also the faculty members have different methods for teaching and instruction where the library helps in identification of sources. The investment of library is multi-folding and multidimensional due to diversity in nature of academic processes and desired results.

INCLUSIVE NATURE OF STRATEGIC PRIORITIES OF LIBRARY

The library plans continuously but the strategies are intense and highly overlapping. The overall planning takes care of various aspects such as moving along with the university's planning of growth in learning and research; enhancing the reputation in international scenario and developing collaboration at national and international level. The accountability in terms of education, research as well as finances, the university library has to cope with the paces of university strategies for a certain period. Whereas the university plans for five years according to financial policies and plans of country, the library plans accordingly but at annual basis including short term plans leading towards long term goals. The achievements are not immediate yet at over a period of time the results are visible. The library functions according to strategic objectives which are roughly as following:

- Pacing with university's growth plan
- Working with close collaboration of faculty members
- Developing support services for specific kinds of users
- Arrangement of temporary suitable solutions for specific kinds of needs of various kinds of users such as increasing time durations of library opening hours
- Understanding the different kinds of users and their needs

- Extending the range of services, developing various means and methods for facilitating access to e-resources, specially understanding the needs for specific kinds of research needs of university as a whole and students at individual level
- Facilitating liaison among faculty members, students and external sources of information supply
- Facilitating the educational partnership at national and international level
- Providing information literacy support to the users of diversified backgrounds
- Meeting goals yet to have sustainable model for development of library programs
- Maintaining the unique identity of library resources, collections and services
- Establishing itself as a highly significant support for learning in the university as well as across the world
- Having strategic option for maintenance and development of specific collections, archiving and access
- Engaging the user community in spread of learning resources from the library as well as the library as a support center for their academic activities
- Concentrating on the past and present weaknesses; identification of the areas for improvement
- Utilization of grants, funds and budgets in timely and effective manner
- Identification of opportunities such as collection building based on demand and needs, collaboration etc.
- Avoiding the new generation threats such as increasing use of ICT and losing touch with users due to more use of virtual or online environment

- Arranging safeguards for library e-resources due to highly volatile policies of publishers, aggregators and other agencies
- Predicting future on the basis of past and current trends of user demands, university policies and the library practices
- Identification of dependencies and enabling the proper sustainable facilities

CONSTANT ENDEAVORS BASED ON NEEDS AND PREPARATION

The library always keeps itself in touch with the academic courses and concerned sources to meet the demands. Whereas there are demands for particular new courses, there is constant updating on the current courses at university. The library provides information sources as well as the instructions on how to access and use these resources. The sources and instruction courses are well designed keeping in view few facets such as the availability, integration into academic programs, needs of users and inclusion of quality methods. The central library always endeavored to maintain the up-to-date information sources with an informative approach. The policies for various kinds of users include facets such as undergraduate and post graduate students, research scholars as well as faculty members. For the various kinds of users, the few significant aspects are as following:

i. Ready access and information about the collection
ii. Maintaining collection, based on the institution's curriculum
iii. Measurement of collection by quality and usage
iv. Provision of reference collections as well as interdisciplinary indexes
v. In-campus as well as off-campus access maintenance

with the sustainable development and revising for the future

vi. Informing the users about various policies and inclusion of them into it

PLANNING FOR THE LIBRARY STAFF

The efficient library staff is the backbone of a good library. Their knowledge, expertise and skills are the tools that build better library services. The library has kinds of staff and various posts in order to serve the readers; some of them keep busy in housekeeping and background services and rest of them do the front desk jobs. The tasks and objectives run in sync because of learned staff. The ability to ensure library services and developments is in the minds and hands of library staff. The following factors are significant to plan the need of staff and assigning of responsibilities:

i. Existing resources and library services

ii. Support staff

iii. User population and diversity

The staff needs following abilities:

i. Instructional methods

ii. Communication skills

iii. Expertise, and flexibility

FACILITIES

The planning of facilities is necessary in order to have an outlet for services. The facilities are significant for collaborative spaces and requirements. To promote the library resources, innovative and attractive infrastructure is required. The interaction building facilities and environment is necessary for a library that needs to connect with each of its user. The facilities are designed and implemented in realization to the following:

i. Opening hours and access to library circulation hours and spaces
ii. Planning of safety and other facilities (fire-fighting facilities, etc.)
iii. Space meeting the needs of academic programs and increasing collaboration among learners
iv. Well-equipped library in context with the networking facilities and other power-charging means

Various other aspects significant in planning are as following:

i. Administration
ii. Budget

The open and well-lit library provides an environment that suits studies. To accelerate the learning, the combination of surrounding niche and academic atmosphere plays a great role. The library building as a physical premise and a learning temple, gives narrations of stories that a learner learns while studying there. The ample times spent in library form a peculiar framework in the minds of students that remain persistent throughout lives. The planning of entire library in a new era follows few guidelines such as:

i. Implementing the technology that enhances facilities
ii. Augmenting the users' interaction
iii. Consulting the building trends which are environment-friendly
iv. Creating accessible spaces and facilities including the identification and location indications
v. Implementing assistive technologies for differently-able users and visually impaired users
vi. Generating and creating "multi-function spaces" to adapt to new demands and situations
vii. To design and have the Interactive spaces that are experiential to explore new possibilities

viii. Supporting the user community engagement to promote library resources and services

REFERENCES

1. Act & Statutes. http://www.jnu.ac.in/RTI/Act%20&%20Statutes/ACT.pdf

2. Alexandra Papazoglou, Eva Semertzaki, (2001) "Changes and developments in Greek libraries", The Electronic Library, Vol. 19 Iss: 3, pp.158 - 167

3. Ali Biranvand, Hadi Sharif Moghaddam, (2013) "Feasibility assessment of creating an inter library loan system and document delivery services in public libraries of Fars Province (Iran)", The Electronic Library, Vol. 31 Iss: 1, pp.24 - 35

4. Amara Malik, Khalid Mahmood, (2013) "Infrastructure needed for digital reference service (DRS) in university libraries: An exploratory survey in the Punjab, Pakistan", Library Review, Vol. 62 Iss: 6/7, pp.420 - 428

5. Amritpal Kaur, (2011) "Impact of electronic journals on university libraries of India: a study", Library Management, Vol. 32 Iss: 8/9, pp.612 – 630

6. B.T. Sampath Kumar, B.S. Biradar, (2010) "Use of ICT in college libraries in Karnataka, India: a survey", Program, Vol. 44 Iss: 3, pp.271 - 282

7. Brad Eden, (2005) "The UNLV Libraries: four years after the construction of a new main library", Library Hi Tech, Vol. 23 Iss: 1, pp.5 - 7

8. David McMenemy, (2009) "Library Technology Companion: A Basic Guide for Library Staff", Program, Vol. 43 Iss: 2, pp.232 - 233

9. Donna Ellen Frederick , (2015) "On eBooks in academic libraries: an article based on a presentation at the Library 2.014 Conference", Library Hi Tech News, Vol. 32 Iss: 5, pp.12 - 15

10. Emil Hudomalj, Avgust Jauk, (2006) "Authentication and authorisation infrastructure for the mobility of users of academic libraries: An overview of developments", Program, Vol. 40 Iss: 1, pp.63 - 73

11. Fan Aihong, (2009) "Creating a bilingual library information environment for foreign users", The Electronic Library, Vol. 27 Iss: 2, pp.237 - 246

12. Faranak Mohsenzadeh, Alireza Isfandyari Moghaddam, (2011)

"Perceptions of library staff regarding challenges of developing digital libraries: The case of an Iranian university", Program, Vol. 45 Iss: 3, pp.346 - 355

13. Graham Matthews , Graham Walton , (2014) "Strategic development of university library space: Widening the influence", New Library World, Vol. 115 Iss: 5/6, pp.237 - 249
14. Jeanne M. Brown, Jennifer L. Fabbi, Cheryl Taranto, (2005) "Branch libraries and technology: impact of a new main library", Library Hi Tech, Vol. 23 Iss: 1, pp.90 - 101
15. JNU Library Website. http://lib.jnu.ac.in/
16. Judy Hodge Sackett, (2001) "Planning the new central academic library", New Library World, Vol. 102 Iss: 6, pp.207 - 210
17. Mapulanga Patrick , (2014) "Prospects and constraints of staff development in the University of Malawi Libraries", The Bottom Line: Managing library finances, Vol. 27 Iss: 1, pp.29 – 41
18. Md Roknuzzaman, Katsuhiro Umemoto, (2009) "How library practitioners view knowledge management in libraries: A qualitative study", Library Management, Vol. 30 Iss: 8/9, pp.643 - 656
19. Michael A. Crumpton, (2012) "Strategic positioning for staff realignment", The Bottom Line, Vol. 25 Iss: 4, pp.143 - 148
20. Mitch Lundquist, Steven C. Daggett, Mark McClung, Peter C. Gorman, (1998) "Section 4: Technical infrastructure of the electronic library", Library Hi Tech, Vol. 16 Iss: 3/4, pp.110 - 124
21. Murle E. Kenerson (2001), The effects of automation on hiring practices and staff allocation in academic libraries in Tennessee, in Edward D. Garten, Delmus E. Williams (ed.) *Advances in Library Administration and Organization (Advances in Library Administration and Organization, Volume 18)* Emerald Group Publishing Limited, pp.175 - 223
22. Nguyen Hong Sinh, Daniel G. Dorner, G.E. Gorman, (2011) "The influence of library manager styles on continuing education of university library practitioners in Vietnam", Library Management, Vol. 32 Iss: 8/9, pp.505 - 515
23. Petros Kostagiolas, Anastasia Margiola, Anastasia Avramidou, (2011) "A library management response model against the economic crisis: The case of public libraries in Greece", Library Review, Vol. 60 Iss: 6, pp.486 - 500
24. Roy Tennant, (2004) "A bibliographic metadata infrastructure for the twenty first century", Library Hi Tech, Vol. 22 Iss: 2, pp.175 – 181

25. Sandie King, David McMenemy, Alan Poulter, (2006) "Effectiveness of ICT training for public library staff in the UK: staff views", The Electronic Library, Vol. 24 Iss: 2, pp.265 - 276

26. Simon Bains, (2000) "Developing a library staff Intranet at City University", VINE, Vol. 30 Iss: 2, pp.48 - 52

27. Sue Samson , Kimberly Swanson , (2014) "Support your staff employees: they support the academy", Reference Services Review, Vol. 42 Iss: 1, pp.165 - 180

28. Ulla Wimmer, (2009) "What do higher education management and administration expect of library benchmarking?: Results of a workshop on BIX – the Library Index for Academic Libraries in Germany", Performance Measurement and Metrics, Vol. 10 Iss: 2, pp.116 - 121

29. Yajie Zhao, (2009) "Changing of library services under e research environment", The Electronic Library, Vol. 27 Iss: 2, pp.342 - 348.

5
The Means of Deliverance and Staffing

The status of staff (in terms of number, the occupying posts and qualifications, abilities, capacities and potentials)

The need and necessity of enormous augmentation in above all attributes of library staff

Identification of areas of immediate concern and futuristic planning

INTRODUCTION

The staff or the human resource of the library is the medium or the bridge between the library resources and library users. The trained library staff is the vehicle to reach the library goals. The training of staff is concerned with library service strategies. The staff should be able to handle the work in any section of the library. The ultimate objective is the ability to handle basic jobs in the library to serve the users' request. There have been programs for staff development in the library. The trainings in context with archiving, open access, digitization and digital libraries are very much in need and taken by the library to make the staff learn and update. JNU Central Library has applied various means and taken different approaches to inculcate the professional training and informal learning.

NEED FOR LIBRARY RESTRUCTURING: HUMAN RESOURCE

The libraries support their organization by the services created to serve the component users. In the academic libraries, the component users are the students, researchers and faculty members. To strengthen the building blocks of the university, the library serves its purpose. Here the question comes in picture: how and why the human resource or the staff of library is instrumental in completing the goals of parent organization.

The way the libraries have followed a system of hierarchy and levels in the internal management is often the compliance of government policy and parent organizational guidelines. Sometimes the system that exists does not function in accordance with the targets a library has set. The JNU library has gone a structural improvement in order to achieve its status as one of the great library of India. The structural improvements are comprised of filling the vacant posts, bringing qualified staff, and continuous motivation to do better. The improvement does not end with the recruitment but leads by allocating the tasks, resources and people to each section meant for specific purpose. The characteristic during the last 2-3 years has been an outcome of rigorous planning to implement staff overhaul in terms of number as well as quality. In this context, the authoritative strategy within JNU administration has been enthusiastic along with the Librarian. The library stands on the pillars of collective efforts of staff and the unity to serve the organization at its best.

The Current Staff

Table 1

University Librarian	*Deputy Librarian*	*Assistant Librarian*	*Professional Assistant*	*Semi Professional Assistant*	*Technical Assistant*	*Library Attendant*
1	3	12	24	20	1	26

(***Source:*** JNU Library Website. http://lib.jnu.ac.in/)

The above table shows the number of staff working currently in the library. The present strength of library staff is the outcome of continuous efforts of Library authority and JNU administration. The staff is given responsibility in various sections designed to meet users' expectations. There are few chosen reasons behind the planning of placing staff in various sections:

i. To keep certain number of staff in one section as is required.

ii. To keep them up to a certain period of time so that they gain efficiency and expertise in the duties assigned.

iii. To make them understand the significance of their job as contribution towards library's goal.

iv. To change their positions by transferring to other sections to train them other responsibilities or as and when the shuffle is required.

v. To let them interact and gain understanding users' attitude by placing in sections directly related with users' services.

The library services and staff always demand attention from each other. The integrity of library depends upon the efficient staff delivering library services. The transformation of library staff into the service provider and; contributing towards organizational productivity supports the library in establishing itself 'the heart of university' as said often. So the reorganizing the human resources in JNU library amends if any mistake has been committed as well paves way for better services for the users.

THE LIBRARY STAFF OFFERS TO CAPACITY BUILDING OF LIBRARY

The library services depend on library staff. The qualifications, knowledge of work, understanding the duties and the targets to be achieved are few but mandatory facets of the entire picture in the mind of a library professional. The clear understanding of staff and their assigned duties are the prerequisite for the beginning of library's journey into the minds of satisfied users. The capacity building through library staff being a continuous process is composed of following components:

i. Constant watch on the users' expectations and possessed skills

ii. Continuous updating of knowledge to impart duties

Capacity developed by the broader vision keeping the library staff in mind has faster and stronger effect in library services. The designing and execution of capacity building of library depends upon the methods employed by staff in imparting their duties. The work done with the objective to serve the library reader is well done, rather than just fulfilling the minimum of the assigned responsibilities. The eye on fulfillment of service goal is much more important than the carrying on the duties. The sustainable status is achieved by continuous and constant endeavors to meet the users' expectations. The success achieved by the JNU library staff has been due to:

i. Vision to meet library users' expectations

ii. Commitment to serve

iii. Support and participation of authorities

The growth and quality of services has been due to going on planning and implementation at various levels. The development takes place through library staff in different ways that constitute the levels on which each individual effort and collective responsibilities are counted for. At the individual level, the learning and training received by the staff created an ambience for better services as well as motivation for other staff to learn and do better. When there are opportunities for enhancing organizational capabilities, the entire section staff is trained and expected to act according to new learning. For example, the implementation of automation software in each section of library and e-office training, turns to enhance the library capacities. In essence, when library formulates a strategy to exercise or design a policy that functions at the highest level that is the library in the capacity of an organization. Various levels of capacities have been separate yet intertwined only to create harmony and uniformity in the library services. The small reforms and the big tasks taken to improve the "human resource capacity" of library have been influential in order to create an arena of library services. The chances have been in the library to motivate and pursue new skills and knowledge. The acquired skills and knowledge supports the resolving the day today situations in a big academic library like JNU. The genesis of innovative and enhanced level of services has been achieved in last two years due to overcoming the fears as well as welcoming the ideas to serve the library users.

There has been improvement and evaluation of following facets of human resource development in JNU library, such as competencies, capabilities and the capacity. The previous discussion talks about various levels of capacities in the library staff at JNU but the emphasis is on developing skills at individual level to absorb in duties. The competencies of individuals are collected to form the capabilities of a group or section to perform the responsibilities. When the competencies and capabilities are joined to achieve organizational goals, they form the capacity of staff in context with the organization itself. The same planning applied to JNU library to create new sections and various kinds of library services. At individual level of the human resource in the library, the planning concentrates at the method of performing duties, relating to other section staff or team member. The aspects such as adaptation and cohesive nature of library staff comes into picture which has been visualized at JNU library.

The Factors for Augmentation of Library Staff In Terms of Number and Skills

The number of people as library staff is hardly sufficient in any library but the means and methods to increase the number depends upon the parent organization's policies as well as efficiency of staff for meeting the goals. The factors for the visible change in JNU library as well as the library staff are:

1. Strong leadership to direct the library staff.
2. Constantly deserting and deleting the past unfruitful practice of staff management.
3. Effective planning and implementation, structure of duties and responsibilities, framed policies and rules.
4. Regular exercises of monitoring and reviewing the overall strategies; actions taken.
5. Continuous encouragement to learn and act.

THE RESTRUCTURING AND RE-ENGINEERING: ROLE OF LIBRARY STAFF

The restructuring as well as the reengineering of services of library depends on understanding of qualitative services provided by the library staff. The restructuring of library services and staff has been done considerably in JNU library due to changed scenario in the library services worldwide. The anticipated as well as projected targets compelled the JNU library to include the modifications in the methods, applied previously in deputing staff for various duties, functions and services. There have been following reasons for reengineering in the "human resource management" at JNU library:

i. Assessment of trends

The leadership in JNU library identified the need to change due to the ongoing trends in the librarianship. Trends have been related with the inclusion of information and communication technologies almost in each area of library housekeeping and services.

ii. Identification of capabilities

The initiation of restructuring goes on with the discovery of areas and suggested capabilities. The knowledge of information technology and interest to adapt accordingly to meet organizational goals has been crucial to become effective in utilization of capabilities.

iii. Active inputs from the past

The in-depth research of the previous processes, methods applied in the library led to create understanding of needed and desired kinds of services. Some of the actions carried on from two-three decades were outdated and few of these were obsolete in the current times. To discard and discontinue these functions or services became mandatory to cope with current requirements.

iv. Search and inclusion of talent in the library staff

During last couple of years, the appointed staff has been found relatively fast learner in context with the new technologies. There have been a number of opportunities and efforts to train the staff and retain the talent in order of meeting users' expectations.

v. Exchange of learning and in-house training

An innovative method to train the fellow staff; when the senior and professionally trained staff taught the practices and procedures to juniors from various sections. This approach gave the library staff a better platform for interaction and learning medium. Also the section authorities could also learn about the fears and dilemma of the subordinate staff concerned with their day-today duties and functions.

vi. Absorption of reengineered status

The rigorous planning and thoughtful implementation of reengineered library could be possible due to active participation, adaptation, time to time training, and absorption of ideas. The construction and maintenance of library website with the goal to inform and provide services to users is one of the examples to reflect reengineered services.

vii. Balancing the change and stability

There have been tremendous endeavors such as to synchronize the functions carried from the past with the newly adopted mechanisms to improve the library services. The responsibilities assigned to senior staff in the traditional services and functions related with changing technologies are to be carried out by the next generation of library staff. The abilities of staff and anticipated duties should match to bring out the desired results in the library services.

POTENTIAL AREAS AND AMBITIONS OF LIBRARY STAFF

Assumption of the areas which require maintenance, management and mending gives a clear insight into the development of library service. For this development the academic library such as JNU library has found out to have distinctive occupation to deal with improvement in the existing methods and service. The previous approaches such as dependence on manual records or seeking supports from outside the organization regarding the technological purposes have been discarded. These approaches were replaced by steps taken by trained staff. One significant area of development has been the opportunity provided to library staff to be vocal about their ideas and ambition "how to add value to the existing system". The staff was motivated to speak their aspirations for improving library services. The identification of potential areas depended on:

i. The willingness of staff
ii. The enthusiasm to augment the quality
iii. The capacity to find out the lacking areas
iv. The presence of capable staff
v. The infrastructural satisfaction
vi. The organizational support

The above noted facets to complete the picture of potential developments in the library, were possible due to library staff and its multidimensional approaches. The directions framed by the library staff and reaching to determined goals in various sections have been few ideas which have been stuck in the minds of people. The coordination among various library sections has been the outcome of understanding of approach comprising redefined interrelation of various functions in the library. The correlation and interdependence of various activities in library required the circulation of resources and continuous flow of deliverance. The existence of managerial issues yet assertion towards reaching to the library goals ventured through patience. The professional interests with desire to gain the status of ultimate service in a particular section give the satisfaction to concerned staff also. The credited values and processes can be classified, here, as:

i. Conceptual values
ii. Predefined and preoccupied capacities
iii. Persuasive performance improvement
iv. Operational efforts
v. Extraction of specifically combined processes and outcomes

The journey taken in development of library staff and library services is a combination of various multifarious endeavors. Whereas the presence of established principles of library staff development, their maximum contribution and ideal environment in library supported the JNU library to contribute in human resource management, the continuous motivating factors, for example, timely promotions among the existing staff paved way for better performance. As the lack of promotional avenues always creates some hesitation and lack of interest in the library staff, this aspect was well taken care of.

LIBRARY STAFF, ORGANIZATION AND LINKING WITH USERS

The library authority and leadership have been quite pursuing the idea to connect the library staff with organizational values and the users' expectations. To create this link there has been an overwhelming research into the previous existing system and the current practices around the places. The library explored the capability to build the relationship among library staff, users and faculty members to create an environment of well connected library and users in niche of value based services. The stepping stones for the triangular contexts are the following ones:

i. Attention to areas of users' services
ii. Creating direct approach to users
iii. Seeking support of faculty members

Continuous involvement of library staff with each dimension of library services and their receivers has been one of the prudent methods. The student community and faculty members have been the external partners of the library staff. The demands, suggestions from the user community by various means to connect with them have been the guiding force for the library staff. The library has been open for the suggestion for the better services because these are the users' needs and expectations which shape the library services. The few aspects related with library staff and users, explain it following way:

i. Creating a plan to network
ii. Understating how to relate with strategies
iii. Sharing the experiences, and criticism
iv. Ability to mobilize the technical support
v. Surrogating the learning facilities

INSTILLED SKILLS IN LIBRARY STAFF

At various levels, the library staff needs different kinds and combinations of skills to perform the responsibilities. The skills are not taught in a library school but developed through insight and willingness. The personal abilities of library staff contribute in his/her positions in the organizational structure of JNU library. Due to augmented responsibilities on higher positions in library, the required skills also combine. For example, while cataloguing a staff person needs only technical knowledge and skills, but the position of in-charge of processing section needs leadership and authoritative skills as well along with managerial skill. At one time, a particular job responsibility demands the skills as well as expectations from the library staff. And there are hardly any chances to decrease in responsibility in library. At the definite circumstance, the position of a library staff needs a number of skills. In general, the common types of skills are needed at entire plane of library positions such as technical skills with conceptual skills, not without the much required human skills. A number of skills are found and instilled in JNU library staff discussed as given:

- Technical Skill
- Presentation Skills
- Time Management Skills
- Leading Skills
- Decision-Making Skills

These stated skills and their combinations have been put together to make the things work miraculously. Looking deep into the skills or any set of skills, it forces to learn that the lower positions or the positions directly in touch with library users require in depth of technical skills rather than the decision making skills. The person working on the position of assistant librarian supposed to have technical skill to keep the work going, the leadership skill to direct the members of section and human skills to let the people work and grow together in a group. As the position moves in hierarchy in the library, a person with particular set of responsibilities needs to work and gets work done by the support of time-management, leadership, and organizational skills. The middle level positions such as senior assistant librarians and deputy librarians do have presentation skills, controlling skills as well as leadership skills. At few occasions, the decision making skills are inadvertent among the senior positions in library. The following list displays the kinds of skills found in generally among the library staff at library:

- Conceptual Skill
- Communication Skills
- Controlling Skills
- Planning Skills
- Organization Skills

PROFESSIONAL COMPETENCIES AMONG LIBRARY STAFF

The job responsibilities require certain professional competencies and sometimes create an opportunity to develop the competencies among library staff. Various positions and the promotions of library staff often demand professional competencies. To perform their duties responsibly and successfully, the possession of competencies paves a smooth way for library staff. The staff at JNU library has been able to handle the responsibilities in varied nature of circumstances with the help of following reasons:

i. personal and professional competencies
ii. technological competencies

There has been visible improvement in the competencies of library staff at various levels and positions due to exposure of ICT and training programs. The competency in a library staff provides opportunities due to content of knowledge and skills leading to serve and result to a threshold of value-added library services. The competencies among the library staff are directly concerned with the knowledge of current as well as retrospective information resources and access. The related technology to manage and enhance the use of the library resources, functions as a tool towards better information services.

The competencies in a library professional help to stand apart and able to serve better. The competent staff at library has been able to understand the complex technologies applied. Their ability to understand and adapt the technology has been a technique to bring the library services at right position and the library itself at elated ground. The installation and presence of competencies have urged the JNU library staff to accomplish their roles as service providers:

i. In challenged environment

ii. Ability to act in the ambience of new technologies

The awareness of new technologies that are not new for a long time means a new day is welcoming another new technology making the job of library staff difficult yet endeavoring to support the library at the same time. With the help of basic skills such as knowledge of operating a computer system, library automation etc., the library staff entered in the work area either with some enhanced size of curiosity or the compulsion of new learning such as scripting languages, working in the online environment. The added knowledge of various intricate services and troubleshooting augment their competencies. Even the senior and old staff in various technical capacities has been trained beyond the earlier knowledge of using search engines, e-mail and database searching. Now the older and young professional staff is able to use various equipments such as scanning devices, printer etc. The day-today use of technology helps them in understanding better use and playing with tools to have comfort of serving. The curiosity and the compulsions tend to force the library staff to learn the new emerging technologies. It is always difficult to cope with the pressure of constantly generated need to deal with technology, as at certain times some of the library staff reflects the difficulty in keeping up with the flow. But to have an expert always related to any new implemented technology helps in training of fellow library staff. The trainings of newly adopted tools and technologies support in keeping with new forces of learning.

The knowledge of computer and information technology is not sufficient to call the library staff competent. The communication skills and ability to serve the library customer have been the competencies in demand always. The value of communication is related with the internal management as well as the library users. The customer oriented library staff at JNU library demonstrates the competencies and contemplates the requirements of more competencies to make JNU library a service oriented organization. The competency of communication has helped in negotiating with publishers, understanding the library users, explaining the library management and everyone else concerned with library. The competencies are reflected in other areas of library management and service provision, certainly other than the technological developments. The absolute combination of competency is completed with the inclusion of assessment ability. Without skills such as evaluation of self (library staff) and the several services, the movement towards better services could not have been possible at JNU library. The focus on the service aspect can refrain itself from the limelight if there is need of concentrating about the needs, skills and willingness of the concerned library staff in a group to create one particular section or service. The coordination among library staff and the university IT staff has been a 'support competency' to create and develop successful services of JNU library. The designing and deliverance of value added information products as well as library services have been possible due to successful use of identified competencies.

The competencies such as knowledge of conceptual skills have been instrumental in the formulation of ideas and implementation of them. The ability to conceptualize the continuously changing and complex situations in JNU library has helped in understanding the crude facts and visualizing the goals to achieve. This creative ability leads to innovation and has been mechanical to put the library objectives forth. The leadership at individual level is combined; and with the knowledge of policies and various standards the library staff has been able to maintain knowledge about current issues each time whenever required. The competencies have helped in:

i. Developing skilled knowledge to serve purpose of the service

ii. Identification of resources which are appropriate to serve library users

iii. Inculcating expertise and ability to assess the developed scenario

iv. To go on with the changes and gain from them by learning and implementing in the library

The library staff has been learning and to manage the acquisition and dissemination in a new light of information technologies. The recent developments and extensive experiments in the library have compelled the library staff to be adept and minimize the time lag. During these developments, the library staff has been efficient in another competency i.e. project management skill.

LIBRARY STAFF AND STRENGTHS

Due to continuous changes in the library world scenario, the development of new services and maintaining the services from the past, the library staff has been on the verge of different thresholds. At one hand carrying on the tradition of routine tasks, on another hand there has been verve of innovation. The library staff has been trained to enhance the services of library as community center. The way, the library staff serves the students and faculty members, has been a bridge between the library users and library. The creation of connections at various levels served to let the library emerge as a community serving organization. The relationship exists between staff and users and it has paved a path for better understanding also, towards developing resources and services. The library has concentrated on the areas where the staff could connect with library users to maximize the interactions. Such activism increases the awareness of library staff and users too. The focused aspects have been:

i. Library outreach

ii. Building partnerships

iii. Training of library staff as well as library users

The library leadership focused on removing the isolation of library staff and users by bringing out means and methods to strengthen the library staff and shaping the attitudes towards the users. The library staff excels at creating interface for the library and users in order to serve the medium or platform for exchange of ideas. The library staff does not exist for providing books merely; to provide information as desired by the users. By connecting the library services knowledge with the recent ICT knowledge, the library staff is functioning for users.

THE GUIDING PRINCIPLES FOR LIBRARY STAFF

Inducing the right motto in the library staff is the strength for the future. Once the JNU library staff has understood the mission of library, the guiding force has been established for a constant supply of information services. These principles guide the library staff to function accordingly in the changed circumstances. The library staff works keeping the purposes in mind such as:

i. subject based learning, based on individual requirements

ii. multidisciplinary approach concerned with entire student community

The staff understands the need of literacy and awareness programs for themselves to have the knowledge of individual students as researcher as well as the students belonging to a class or program. The library functions as a hub for the learners which is the outcome of rigorous testing in various times and circumstances similar to changing users' demands, their choices of media as well as opening of new courses at JNU. There have been tremendous efforts to understand the deficiency in collections of various subjects. The library staff has a clear understanding of working as information facilitators. How to lead the users towards reading materials is different from them reaching to the reference collections. The guiding principles have been inspired from:

i. Library users' needs
ii. Organizational culture to enhance the learning
iii. Interactive sessions with the students
iv. Creating accessible platforms and resources

How the guiding circumstances have been framed is the question of timeless learning for the library staff; the role of changing information scenario, need of flexible policies and inclusions of more activities to catalyze the information service. To reach to desired goals of serving the users has been a chase after the information technologies in the routine processes to make the library operations less cumbersome and more modern. The provision of instant access to library resources due to changing perceptions of library users has been another guiding parameter in the JNU library. Keeping in mind the generation gap of library users as well as library facilities have played a sincere role in finding out the areas to serve more. The matter of identity among the library users has never been a problem for the library. The interactive and active library staff became instrumental to create a new identity of library among the student; where they find the information for the cause of learning.

THE LIMITATIONS AND THE VICTORS

The present status of library regarding the services and its place among the users has been the outcome of continuous victory over the hurdles library faced a couple of years back. The library has been fortunate to have the leadership that changed those hurdles into the opportunities and possibilities of new avenues for experiences. Whenever there has been crisis for accommodating contemporary technologies and carrying current practice, the staff felt pushed or too motivated to include each facet of librarianship. The limitations of time and physical space compelled the library staff to face new boundaries within which the staff has to serve at the best. Since each staff member cannot be assigned the burden of expectation, the staff was trained and taught to serve the people whose steps are falling in their section or asking for the services directly related with their duties. It is better to find out the needs of user and the library staff prepares itself to serve them. Far from being a silent zone, the library staff made it possible to create the library into an interactive place. The library staff now sees various methods to help the library users. The digital initiatives and the online platforms have paved another way to reach to users. The library staff became proactive and began to reach to the every user of library. The demands of users are different, the processes vary yet the purpose of library staff is same i.e. to serve the users. The means and promotions to cater library services have been influenced by encouraging the users to visit library in person and by online medium. The limitations faced by library staff have been overcome by the creating library's face in online world. The alterations in the working layout have also been a means of recovering from the previous problems. The explorations to organize library resources and services happened by means of identification of barriers towards use of the same. The concept of seclusion of library staff from the library users and isolation of them from the newly incorporated services was obsolete and an impediment in the purpose. Understanding the problems such as the classification system in the perspective of users as well as directing towards the electronic platform or remote access is few of the examples those have been dealt very carefully in JNU library. The focus on library users' problems has made the library staff, a vivid learner.

INNOVATIONS AND LIBRARY STAFF

The library staff has been follower of inventions, innovations and invitations to join them and become part of the library's journey. The time has witnessed the possibility of continuous development in the library through the participation of library staff and embracing the innovations. The innovations have happened in the form of digital revolution. The arrival of books in electronic format and the timely presence of journals have been few matter of curiosity as well as surprise for the library staff. The excitement of digital information sources and services posed itself sometimes like a forced education on a reluctant child but the library staff considered and took as a ladder to reach in a better ambience. Though the library staff tends to be on both sides of library development but there is debate about the extent of inclusion of modern technologies in the housekeeping functions and services.

The provision of 'single window search' or the display of new arrivals on library website involves efforts and gives a technological pleasure of being on web to the library staff. When the library informs a new user about the remote access, a sense of pride is reflected that library is able to serve beyond its walls. The out-of-box information services gain superiority over the traditional methods. The technological innovations lead the library to change the perception among the library users and support the library to offer most modern kind of services. A library website with full of systematic links to resources, services and points of interaction becomes the outcome of adaptation of innovation by the library staff. Utilization of technology to keep the library users informed is one of the adept purposes of innovation. Time saving techniques for the users is the benefits of innovation in the JNU library.

Generation of few services that provide a platform for collaboration and the increased use of library space and facilities by innovating services have happened during last 2-3 years. The 'JNU Forum for Mutual Learning, scanning for research documents, plagiarism check are few of the services in which the library staff and library users are directly involved. Such instances provide opportunities to understand the library users' demands. The idea of more services and more interaction intrigues the library staff yet there has not been less charm of innovating or welcoming new services in the library. The role of library staff and innovation are intricately woven. The library staff provides the place for learning to students what they could have missed in the classroom. Due to changed attitude, the library has become a place of creation, besides finding collection for reading. The direction of users towards library has been conventional but the innovation paved way of information towards the users. The optimism in the library leadership in the staff has played a great role in absorbing the thought of innovation. Informing and providing tools for creativity and learning is lateral face of innovation in JNU library.

The thrill lies in providing more number of equipments to use and improved version of library services through services such as support for visually impaired students. Here, example of expansion of library space for readers is worth mentioning. Due to technological advances, the library is reaching 24/7 to users. Apart from digital innovation, the role of library staff is quite prominent in document delivery services (DDS) where the personal contacts play very crucial role. Due to courteous nature and professional attitude, the library staff is able to serve a good number of readers. The communication skills have been supporting to reach to greater number of readers, also enhancing the reputation of library as a serving organization. The response from the served readers at the required time is always overwhelming, thus functioning as motivator for the library.

ROADBLOCKS AND CONCERNS

The ideal library services are dependent on efficient library staff and the sufficient amount of deliberations. There are issues such as lack of time or uncoordinated manpower but the continuous developments in terms of appointing the staff in library has been a matter of great concern. The implementation of library planning and services requires administrative efforts too. The deliverance of services is related with service oriented mindset and exploring the options to meet the users expectations. The kind of services library planned has been completely designed keeping in view the library users' needs and a verve to serve them. The university authorities were constantly informed and pursued for human resource planning in the library. Without administrative support and actions, the library could not have been able to appoint the sufficient number of staff in various capacities and positions.

The hesitation at any point of having the sanctioned number of staff in different posts could be a result of reluctance but the continuous pushing towards appointing the approved staff proved a step in right direction. To make any change in library service or initiate a new one requires a positive and welcoming approach by the staff. Any repercussions that occur should be taken as stepping stones. These concerns have been as:

i. Keeping up with the latest technology

ii. Identification of potential innovations

iii. Protecting the user privacy

iv. Reshaping the library role

To deliver the service, there has been persistent activeness in context of:

i. Need of library staff to be more knowledgeable about the digital contents and services.

ii. Dealing with the equipments, information products and the processes.

iii. Understanding the demand and availability of information.

The necessity to keep changing and adapting is the first rule of survival among the fast paced librarians. The staff is also pushed and sometimes this is passed to library users also. When library implements a new service or purchases a new information product, the library staffs as well as users are supposed to use these techniques in order to acquaint themselves with the newly accommodated information product and services. The need of acquaintances and practices on the newly acquired information product or service is considered as a demand of time which always keeps moving. The authoritative support, librarians' responsibilities and the constant push of users' expectations keep the concerns alive to implement an innovative idea.

THE SUPPORT STAFF IN LIBRARY

There are various cadres and positions in the Library System; JNU library follows various rules and U. G. C. Guidelines for the recruitment and promotions of library staff. The support staff is present in JNU library working on various posts as following:

i. Professional Assistants

ii. Semi-Professional Assistants

iii. Library Attendants

The persons working in the above noted positions are responsible to perform various operations in different sections. Their involvement is stated in following means:

i. performing assigned duties/tasks

ii. imparting the routine activities

iii. contributing in specific services

Sometimes the support staff functions in different capacities involving the complexities of duties in varied ranges. The support staff supervises other junior staff and keeps in direct touch with the students also. The assigned duties and tasks of support staff in JNU library are designed in a way which meet the library's goals and organizational aims. The support staff is professionally qualified and trained. The qualifications possessed by these personnel are Bachelor of Library and Information Science (B. L. I. Sc.) and Master of Library and Information Science (M. L. I. Sc.); also the senior staff working in these capacities has the certificates/ degrees as required. The professionally qualified support staff also reaches to senior positions in library by enhancing their qualifications and through promotions. Their skills and experience are always supporting in managing the library operations. In JNU library, during last 2-3 years a great care has been taken in recruiting the professional and semi-professional assistants.

Specifying their Positions

There are various positions which are called in designations as:

- Professional Assistant
- Semi-professional Assistant
- Library Assistant
- Library Technician
- Library Technical Assistant
- Cataloguer
- Classifier
- Library Information Specialist
- Audio Visual Technician

These support staff are recruited to perform various duties and operations, for example, helping in acquiring the books, dealing with membership of students. The following sections run with the help of professional and semi professional assistants:

i. Library membership section
ii. Circulation Section
iii. Acquisitions Section
iv. Processing Section
v. Readers' Services

In fact, no section of library can function without efficient contribution of support staff.

STRENGTH OF SUPPORT STAFF

The professionally competent support staff has the collective ability to run different sections in a very coordinated way. The combinations of skills support to perform the duties in various capacities and they add the value to operations. The performance of assigned duties at individual level contributes towards the sectional achievements. Their professional education and skills enable them doing their duties with sufficient effectiveness and cautiousness simultaneously. Their time-bound output is the result of following attributes:

i. Professional attitudes
ii. Ability for optimal use of resources
iii. Creating strategies to follow and fit in the time frame
iv. Skills of specific kinds to perform their duties
v. Coordinating in complex aspects of human behaviors
vi. Ability to adapt the highly changing information system

The basic as well as significant factor is to adhere to organizational vision with a strategy to focus on library management. There are various functions which are being performed by the support staff. The support staff has skills such as appropriate information management skills and capacity development skills at JNU library. The support staff handles technically the work of library through the well organized resources while keeping the ways of services in mind. The library does not emphasize upon accumulating the resources but how the users can be approached to use these resources. The movement 'of and within' the knowledge world has been drastically changing as well as improving the methods of serving the users. The continuous refreshment of learning and improvement of qualifications among the library staff has proven the basic idea of library's role. The professional assistants along with the semi-professional assistants bring the proficiency in the work. At the same time the professional assistants make learn them the practices of various services with varied methods under different circumstances. The fundamental objective as well as the technique remains same but the information realm brings opportunities to explore methods which have not been conventional or tried before. The personal touch to information services through the direct interaction with students has created the buzz of user friendly library staff. This kind of interaction facilitates the understanding of students' problems concerned with recommendations of books as well as utilization of services. The mechanisms related with acquiring of books or placing the services before the users have certainly been altered if compared with the practices of earlier than last 3-4 years. The public display of library practices is visualized and has been possible due to constant deliberations of professional staff.

When the session begins with the admission of new students into library, it initiates with the developments of courteous and professional behavior of staff. While the user orientation ends within 3-4 days, the library staff continuously supports the understanding of library resources and services throughout the year. The professional staff has been instrumental in creating a platform to bring the library users and services together. The vitality of library solely depends on the supervision of library leadership, coordination of professionals and the vision to be followed. The high priority of meeting the user expectations has been an outcome of sound decisions. The sustenance of prioritized services belongs to meeting the anticipated demands of library users. The strategies to strengthen the research support to users are one of the aspects related with users' services. The entire strategy revolves around the following areas which have been thoroughly taken care:

i. Scheduling the tasks
ii. Assigning the responsibilities and subordination
iii. Rationalizing the finances
iv. Identifying the resources and resource persons in-house

The support staff has invested the time towards the capacity building for the right practices to achieve the organizational goals. The efforts refer to enabling the coordinated and developmental objectives of the library services by the professionally conducted duties and responsibilities. The library staff has taken the community based information services into their routine as designed by the library leadership. The operating efficacies lead to enhanced analytical processes and provide ample platforms for displaying the competitiveness of library authority as well as the professionally trained support staff. Certainly it involves the modified operating procedures and restructuring of staff as well as the sections in the library. The responsibilities and services were divided into two levels such as middle level management and lower level management if that can easily be framed in case of Deputy Librarians and Assistant Librarians respectively. The responsibilities delegated to deputy librarians are as following:

i. Reader Services including membership, circulation services

ii. Acquisition and collection development

iii. Journals; collection and services

iv. Research related services such as Literature Search, Referencing Tools, JNU Forum for Mutual Learning, Library Orientation, Plagiarism etc.

Various responsibilities and services are allocated among the Assistant Librarians are given as following:

i. Thesis and Dissertation section

ii. Management section; Administrative and Management

iii. Science collection; Natural Science, Technology, Computing etc.

iv. Newspaper archiving section

v. Reader Service, membership, circulation

vi. Acquisition Section

vii. Afro-Asian Language Section

viii. Government/UN Publication and Plagiarism Section

ix. Research and training

x. Automation Section

The services have been designed for the following collections:

- Social Science Collections
- Science Collections
- Afro Asian Languages
- European Language
- Russian Collection
- Government Collection
- Special Collections
- Online Databases
- Online Journals
- Print Journals

- Bound Volumes
- Donation / Gift
- Theses and Dissertations

In addition to this, the Management Section looks after the Allocation of Funds and disbursement for the purposes such as:

i. Journals and Books
ii. Library Stationary
iii. Binding of Documents
iv. Minor Repair
v. Contingency and other recurring
vi. Library Furniture and Equipments
vii. Computer Systems

The Management Section of Library functions as establishment or human resource management section of library in a way taking care of:

i. Personal files of Library Staff
ii. Leave Record
iii. Conduct Workshop and Seminars
iv. Bills related jobs

REFERENCES

1. Anna Koulikourdi, (2008) "Library services for people with disabilities in Greece", Library Review, Vol. 57 Iss: 2, pp.138 - 148
2. Arja Juntunen, Ari Muhonen, Ulla Nygrén, Jarmo Saarti (2013), Reinventing the Academic Library and Its Mission: Service Design in Three Merged Finnish Libraries, in Anne Woodsworth, W. David Penniman (ed.) *Mergers and Alliances: The Wider View (Advances in Librarianship, Volume 36)* Emerald Group Publishing Limited, pp.225 - 246
3. Aubrey Harvey Chaputula, (2011) "Impact of the global economic crisis on academic libraries in Malawi: A case study of University of Malawi and Mzuzu University libraries", Library Management, Vol. 32 Iss: 8/9, pp.565 – 578

4. Aubrey Harvey Chaputula, (2012) "State, adoption and use of ICTs by students and academic staff at Mzuzu University, Malawi", Program, Vol. 46 Iss: 4, pp.364 - 382

5. Basil Enemute Iwhiwhu, Elvis Ovietobore Eyekpegha, (2009) "Digitization of Nigerian university libraries: From technology challenge to effective information delivery", The Electronic Library, Vol. 27 Iss: 3, pp.529 - 536

6. Brendan Eze Asogwa , (2014) "Libraries in the information age: A measure of performance, competencies and constraints in academic libraries in Nigerian universities", The Electronic Library, Vol. 32 Iss: 5, pp.603 - 621

7. Chang Chiao-Chen , (2013) "Library mobile applications in university libraries", Library Hi Tech, Vol. 31 Iss: 3, pp.478 - 492

8. Christina Flemming, (2012) "A joint university library: vision and reality", Library Management, Vol. 33 Iss: 1/2, pp.95 - 103

9. Debra Rosenfeldt, (2006) "*Libraries Building Communities: The Vital Contribution of Victoria's Public Libraries*", Performance Measurement and Metrics, Vol. 7 Iss: 3, pp.185 - 192

10. Diane L. Velasquez (2010), Impact of technology on organizational change in public libraries: a qualitative study, in Williams Delmus E., Golden Janine (ed.) *Advances in Library Administration and Organization (Advances in Library Administration and Organization, Volume 29)* Emerald Group Publishing Limited, pp.107 – 183

11. Emmanuel E. Baro, (2010) "A survey of digital library education in library schools in Africa", OCLC Systems & Services: International digital library perspectives, Vol. 26 Iss: 3, pp.214 - 223

12. Fakkirappa Kattimani Shivaputrappa , R. Naik Ramesh , (2013) "Evaluation of librarianship and ICT skills of library and information professionals working in the engineering college libraries in Karnataka, India: a survey", Program: electronic library and information systems, Vol. 47 Iss: 4, pp.345 – 369

13. Holley Long, (2012) "End user development of digital collection mash ups: A survey to assess the suitability of current infrastructure", OCLC Systems & Services: International digital library perspectives, Vol. 28 Iss: 4, pp.199 - 207

14. Janet McCue, (1994) "Technical services and the electronic library: Defining our roles and divining the partnership", Library Hi Tech, Vol. 12 Iss: 3, pp.63 - 70

15. JNU Library Website. http://lib.jnu.ac.in/

16. John Walsh, (2008) "The Effects of Library Orientations on Student Usage of the Library", Library Hi Tech News, Vol. 25 Iss: 1, pp.27 - 29

17. Judi Briden, Ann Marshall, (2010) "Snapshots of laptop use in an academic library", Library Hi Tech, Vol. 28 Iss: 3, pp.447 - 453

18. Kevin Miles, (1996) "Outsourcing in private law libraries since the Baker & McKenzie action", The Bottom Line, Vol. 9 Iss: 2, pp.10 - 13

19. LiLi Li, (2006) "Leveraging quality web based library user services in the digital age", Library Management, Vol. 27 Iss: 6/7, pp.390 - 400

20. Linda Sheridan, (2009) "Harnessing time: empowering staff in the workplace", Library Management, Vol. 30 Iss: 6/7, pp.369 - 382

21. Vinh The Lam, (1999) "Issues in library development for Vietnam", Asian Libraries, Vol. 8 Iss: 10, pp.371 – 379

22. Lizanne Payne, (2005) "Depositories and repositories: changing models of library storage in the USA", Library Management, Vol. 26 Iss: 1/2, pp.10 -17

23. Lynne Brindley, (2006) "Re defining the library", Library Hi Tech, Vol. 24 Iss: 4, pp.484 - 495

24. Magnus Torstensson, (2002) "Libraries and society – the macrostructural aspect of library and information studies", Library Review, Vol. 51 Iss: 3/4, pp.211 – 220

25. Margarita Moreno, Anne Xu, (2010) "The National Library of Australia's document supply service: a brief overview", Interlending & Document Supply, Vol. 38 Iss: 1, pp.4 - 11

26. Milan Ojsteršek , Janez Brezovnik , Mojca Kotar , Marko Ferme , Goran Hrovat , Albin Bregant , Mladen Boroviè , (2014) "Establishing of a Slovenian open access infrastructure: a technical point of view", Program: electronic library and information systems, Vol. 48 Iss: 4, pp.394 – 412

27. Mapulanga Patrick , (2013) "Digitising library resources and building digital repositories in the University of Malawi Libraries", The Electronic Library, Vol. 31 Iss: 5, pp.635 - 647

28. Margaret Davies, (2001) "Creating a virtual reference library: experiences at Suffolk Libraries and Heritage", Program, Vol. 35 Iss: 1, pp.43 - 56

29. Mayank Yuvaraj , (2015) "Cloud libraries", Library Hi Tech News, Vol. 32 Iss: 8, pp.19 - 23

30. Miroslaw Gorny (2009), From the old-fashioned library to the public library: Changes in the cultural functions of Polish academic libraries, in William Graves, James M. Nyce, Janine Golden, Delmus E. Williams (ed.) *Advances in Library Administration and Organization (Advances in Library Administration and Organization, Volume 27)* Emerald Group Publishing Limited, pp.109 – 122

31. Okon E. Ani, Margaret B. Edem, Eno J. Ottong, (2010) "Analysis of internet access and use by academic staff in the University of Calabar, Calabar, Nigeria", Library Management, Vol. 31 Iss: 7, pp.535 - 545

32. Olayinka Catherine Fatoki, (2005) "Prospects of GSM technology for academic library services", The Electronic Library, Vol. 23 Iss: 3, pp.266 - 273

33. Peter Edward Sidorko, (2007) "Fostering innovation in library management and leadership: The University of Hong Kong Libraries Leadership Institute", Library Management, Vol. 28 Iss: 1/2, pp.5 – 16

34. Seema Vasishta, (2013) "Dissemination of electronic journals: A content analysis of the library websites of technical university libraries in North India", The Electronic Library, Vol. 31 Iss: 3, pp.278 - 289

35. Susan A Henricks, Genevieve M. Henricks-Lepp , (2014) "Multiple constituencies model in the identification of library effectiveness", Library Management, Vol. 35 Iss: 8/9, pp.645 - 665

36. Tandi Lwoga Edda, (2014) "Integrating Web 2.0 into an academic library in Tanzania", The Electronic Library, Vol. 32 Iss: 2, pp.183 – 202

37. Tina Budzise Weaver, Jiangping Chen, Mikhaela Mitchell, (2012) "Collaboration and crowdsourcing: The cases of multilingual digital libraries", The Electronic Library, Vol. 30 Iss: 2, pp.220 – 232

38. Xiaoping Sheng, Lin Sun, (2007) "Developing knowledge innovation culture of libraries", Library Management, Vol. 28 Iss: 1/2, pp.36 – 52.

6
Services on Parallel Wheel

Insights and intuitions (the ideas)
New services
Why: to modernize, satisfy library users and give them a feel of a place where they really belong

INTRODUCTION

The modernity of library is infused with the continuous evolvement of technological developments. The tools offered to academic users mechanize and control the process of library services. The vitality that contributes to the academic library services is new yet conventional in array of effectiveness. In general, the library offers innovative tools and services, such as:

- EZproxy
- Content Access and provider
- "Research Library Partnership"
- Discovery Services
- Databases and knowledge base
- Interlibrary Loan for Print and E-books

The trouble begins with the non-availability or problems in accessing the electronic resources. The journey begins with the users' search and ends with a satisfied result of downloadable e-books or journal articles. The easy access to resources is an important key in an academic library to keep the readership intact. The delivery and seamless access to e-resources need various actions as solutions to day-today problems of academic users. How such access is created, revolves around the following aspects:

i. Enhancing the visibility

The broad visibility of resources is must. There needs to be those tools that are supporting the discovery of library resources. The use of union catalogues can be helpful.

ii. Minimizing the responding time

The library identifies gaps in communication process and by bridging it meets the users' needs. It becomes easier to find out the authorized and authentic remedy. There are certain big steps like hosted access and assigning duty to resident technical person etc. which are helpful in improving the troubleshooting at library.

iii. The increased access to content available outside the library

There should be provisions for making those books available to the users which are not part of JNU library collection. The policies, strategies and actions towards a unanimous approach are the solution of this problem. Obviously this is related with inter library loan (ILL), the students and faculty members need resources that are related to their academic pursuits but not found in the organizational library.

The communications with other libraries, the professional attitude and a willingness to serve the academic users are definitely very significant components of ILL program. The more JNU library extends its reach, the bigger numbers of users are served.

iv. Hassle-free access to resources

The visibility of library resources, the inclusive nature of OPAC and smiling staff are few areas that required many efforts from the library leadership. The choice of software, library interface, and delivery of electronic content by the interactive website were the areas of concern to be achieved as soon as the readers' whim for more.

v. The entire world is local

Due to fast changing technology and developments taking place every other day, the visibility and accessibility of resources, publication and reach is worldwide. The students want what is available anywhere at prime, and at the same time they need to showcase their academic output with the help of library. The Institutional Repositories (IR) and Electronic Theses and Dissertation Systems (ETDS) are the examples of this kind of approach.

vi. Combating the library routine

The inclusion of modern techniques in library management, having nicely put work-flows and strict application of framed strategies are the methods to have a simple environment of library. The staff and student interact to find out the implicit search expressions to identify and locate the resources in the print collections as well as the electronic arena.

What are the factors that infuse a modernization in a library? This quest is eternal for an enthusiast in library modernization because the modernity depends on various needs, availability of technology and implementation of planning. The areas where the modernization plays great role are given as following:

i. Library services

An interactive face of library i.e. the website as well as nice reception in the physical premises. There are various purposes and kinds of users for whom the information is sought. Another aspect is that how users can access library, various methods, and resources; and utilize the collection and services in the best manner. The resources and services may also be listed in a way that is easily accessible to the users. There is option of placing all the services confined to "A-Z" that makes easy to understand for the novice users.

ii. Identification and location of resources

It is important to have an option to find out an information desk and an electronic "Library Search" or "Discovery Services". The provision of reading lists as well as subject guides support the identification of library resources related to particular subject areas. The locating tools in physical library are not enough, the digital scenario of library also needs such tools as may be sufficient for the different kinds of users and vast variety of resources.

Identifying the research needs and separate provisions to locate and access these resources are very essential. The library collects special sources of information and maintain but the access to such resources is very much required.

How the JNU library strived for provisions of direct approach between library and users: the following list reflects the activities by which there is direct communication and collaboration between user and library:

- Borrowing of books/documents
- Book Reserving facility by library automation software
- Interlibrary loan Services for meeting the needs of users
- Copying/Printing facility for the readers
- Study Spaces, various reading halls with modern facilities

- Instructions, rules and implementation of regulation for better environment
- Media Services and Training Labs for the students specially to enhance the role in their leaning
- Institutional Repository to showcase the research output of JNU researchers
- Digital Services to give a world-class library services
- Request/recommending Purchase to understand and maximize the role of library users in collection building
- 'Ask the Librarian' service so that the library leadership and authorities are well informed and able to serve the user community

VARIOUS SERVICES IN VOGUE, WORLDWIDE

The incarnations of library services, the emergence and kinds of services are motivated by users' demand and expectations. To summarize and gauge the library services in modern environment, the services can be listed as following:

- Access to online resources
- Accessibility
- Library account
- Application forms
- Borrowing books
- Catalogue
- Charges/fines
- Code of conduct
- Collection development strategy
- Contacting Library Services
- Databases
- Dissertations/Theses
- Document delivery service

- E-books
- E-journals
- Enquiries
- Feedback
- Inter library loans
- International students
- Journals
- Library user guides
- Maps
- Microform Collection
- Newspapers/news access services
- Photocopying services
- Recommend a book
- Reference services
- Remote Access
- Research resources
- Scanning service
- Special Collections
- Subject liaison librarians
- Training
- Visitors

The library has designed services keeping the users in mind i.e. the students and the faculty members. Certain services are for the students, and few are meant for faculty members. The division of services is not clearly demarcated yet the distinction can be made easily.

FEW GLIMPSES FROM JNU CENTRAL LIBRARY: THE SERVICES

The services are associated with tools, techniques and interfaces. The library has created a group of services which are readily available through website. The quest of user begins with the identification and searching of documents and ends with finding these resources.

i. Online Catalogue

The library webpage invites users through OPAC and library catalogue. The user can login, search the "heading search", and save the titles in cart. The user can clear session. The news clippings can also be searched. The user can use advanced search option also. The library catalogue (Web OPAC) facilitates searching, and identification throughout 24x7. Users can search Books, Articles, Journals and Theses etc. Various search options are available such as Quick Searching, Browsing and searching at advanced level also.

In the cart the user can save bibliographic records and copies. The search history provides features such as: time, search, type, refined by, sorted by, filtered by and the results.

The modern services of library are described as following:

- Data Portal
- Electronic Resources
- ETDs
- Institutional Repository
- Open Access
- Press Clippings
- Remote Access
- Single Window Search
- Subject Gateway
- Trial Resources

ii. Single Window Search

The "single window search" has facilities such as browsing throughout the collection, advanced searching, linking to external databases, and to close the session. It facilitates "quick search" through all kinds of documents, or any specific one. Discovery Service uses keywords to search across JNU Library databases and catalogues for books. It includes the collection of e-books, links to articles, available theses as well as audio/video files. This facilitates the search in Full-Text (online), Scholarly (Peer Reviewed) and 'Catalog Only' also.

The following features are available:

- A to Z Search
- Articles
- Books & E-books
- E-Thesis to ETD
- JNU Catalogue
- My Library
- Newspaper Clippings
- Search All

Few Search Guides are available:

- Create Search Alert Guide
- Discovery Service search guide
- EBSCO eBooks Search Guide
- EBSCO eBooks downloading Guide
- EBSCO eBooks iPad Download
- EDS Result List Guide

iii. E-resources

The electronic resources are available in the form of:

a. ***Databases*** : There are online Databases; JNU & UGC-Infonet and World Bank Open Data. The list of JNU and UGC-Infonet databases is given as:

ACM Digital

American Chemical Society

American Institute of Physics (AIP)

American Physical Society

American Society for Microbiology (ASM)

Annual Reviews

ArtStor-2014

BBC Monitoring Library

Cambridge Crystallographic Data Centre (CCDC)

Cambridge University Press

CEIC Macroeconomic Database

China National Knowledge Infrastructure (CNKI)

De Gruyter (Walter de Gruyter GmbH)

Ebsco international Bibliography of Theatre & Dance with Full Text

Ebsco International Security & Counter Terrorism Reference Center

EBSCO Research Database

Ebsco ScoINDEX with Full Text

Ebsco- Applied Science & Technology Source

Ebsco- Humanities Source

Economic and Political weekly

Economic Outlook

Economist Intelligence Unit (EIU)-Country Reports

Emerald Insight

English Historical Documents Online

Foreign Broadcast information services Daily report (FBIS)

Grammarly

Hein Online

HST Biomed & Life Sci. Collection

IEL Online (IEEE Xplore)

Inderscience Online Journals

Indian Citation Index

Indiastat.com

Institute for Studies in Industrial Development (ISID)

Institute of Physics

Integrum Profile

Intellect Journals

J-Gate Custom Content for Consortium (JCCC)

Journal Citation Report (JCR)

JSTOR

Lecture Notes in Computer Science

Lexis-Nexis

Manupatra-Online

MathSciNet

Nature Research Journals

Newspaper Direct

Oxford University Press

Portland Press

Proceedings of the National Academy of Science USA

Project Euclid

Project Muse

ProQuest - Digital National Security Archive (DNSA)

ProQuest - Dissertation and Theses Global

ProQuest Academic Research Library

ProQuest Historical Newspapers Times of India Archive (1838-2004)

ProQuest Historical Newspapers: The Guardian (1821-2003) and The Observer (1791-2003)

ProQuest Historical Newspapers: The Wall Street Journal (1889-1996)

PROQUEST- Literature Online with MLA

Prowess

Royal Society of Chemistry

SAGE Humanities and Social Science (HSS) Package

Sci. Finder Sub Structural Module

Science Direct

Science Magazines : American Association for the Advancement of Science

SciFinder

SCOPUS

SIAM Locus

South Asia Archive

Springer Link

TAIR Database

Taylor & Francis

Thompson Innovations

TOI Archive

Turnitin

Web of Science

Westlaw

Wiley Online Library

WILEY – LAB Protocols

World Bank E-Library

Yearbook of International Organizations

b. ***Online Journals*** **:** The online journals are accessed through website and these are listed at http://lib.jnu.ac.in/Online_Journals in alphabetical manner.

c. ***E-Books*** **:** A big collection of electronic books has been developed during last couple of years. Various e-books providers, aggregators, platforms and publishers are available on library website where the users access the e-books collection.

d. ***E-Newspapers*** **:** The collection of e-newspapers is vast, in fact began long ago. The digitization as well as online subscription of newspapers/services has been supporting. The details are as following:

- *Newspaper Direct (Press Display)* : This Database contains a big number (2990) of full content newspapers and magazines. This information is related from 100 countries. It launches "PressReader Windows Store App". On JNU Intranet/Wi-Fi and through mobile phone it can be accessed by 24/7.
- *North Korea News* : It provides primary and secondary data related with North Korea. It is customized for researchers and academic users.
- *New York Times* : To access this source, NYTimes.com/GroupPass passes are claimed. It is accessible by connected to the university's IP. The user needs to register for NYTimes.com account.
    - *Proquest Newspapers Collection* : This collection has historical newspaper for access. In this collection the available newspapers are "The Guardian" (from 1821 to 2003) and "The Observer" "(from 1791 to 2003)", "The Wall Street Journal" (from 1889 to 1996), "Times of India Archive" (from 1838 to 2004) and the collection of old Urdu newspaper Al-Islah.

The following table displays various newspapers (and the hyperlinks) provided by the library:

- Ajit
- Amar Ujala

- Anand Bazar Patrika
- Asian Age
- Assam Tribune
- Business Bhaskar (Hindi)
- Business Standard : http://www.business-standard.com/india/
- http://epaper.business-standard.com/bsepaper/login.php Daily Awam

Foreign Newspapers

- China Daily
- Island Daily
- Japan Times
- Jerusalem Post
- LE-monde
- Renmin Ribao
- Observer (London)
- Sunday Times (London)

Regional Newspapers

- Asomiya Pratidin
- Etemaad
- Inquilab
- Munsif

Daily Excelsior

- Dainik Assam
- Dainik Bhaskar
- Dainik Jagran
- Deccan Chronicle
- Deccan Herald
- Deshbandhu
- Dinamani

- Economic Times
- Eenadu
- Financial Express
- Financial Times
- Hindu (Chennai)
- Hindu (Delhi)
- Hindustan Times
- Hindustan Times (Hindi)
- Indian Express
- Jansatta
- Loksatta
- Mathrubhumi
- Nai Dunia
- Nav Bharat Times
- Pioneer
- Prajavani
- Rajasthan Patrika
- Rashtriya Sahara (Hindi)
- Roznama Rashtriya Sahar(Urdu)
- Samaj

v. Remote login

To provide information service to the remote places and facilitate in remote access, this services is very popular among library users. The users are provided a login id and password to access e-resources from remote areas i.e. outside the library LAN also. The remote access is Gateway of JNU E-Resources. There are two facilities such as:

i. EZproxy at http://ezproxy.jnu.ac.in/login

ii. MyAthens

MyAthens Services are listed as following:

1. All OpenAthens services
2. OpenAthens MD Single Sign-On service
3. MyAthens user portal
4. OpenAthens Account Administration website
5. Account bulk upload administration service
6. Administration Area statistics reporting
7. OpenAthens API
8. MyAthens self-registration services
9. Customised self-registration services
10. OpenAthens Federation
11. OpenAthens Federation Manager
12. OpenAthens SP Dashboard
13. OpenAthens Proxy services
14. OpenAthens Documentation website
15. OpenAthens Downloads website
16. OpenAthens DSP Administration website
17. OpenAthens Service Desk
18. OpenAthens Service Desk web interface
19. OpenAthens Telephone Support
20. OpenAthens Yum Repository
21. Email services
22. ESDU data service

vi. Trial resources

Time to time, there are resources placed on trial (access for trial basis) for the library users. This trial access to various resources is for review and demand purpose. The few resources on trial access are given as following:

- Bloomsbury Collections
- De Gruyter E-books
- Encyclopedia of Britannica

- Financial Times
- Future-Science
- InCites - Research Analytics
- Keesings World News
- Nature Plants
- Now Publishers
- OECD iLibrary
- Sage Publications
- Sage Research Methods
- SciVal Suite

vii. Data Portal

The data portal helps in accessing the data, produced and published by government agencies like Government of India, State Governments, United Nations Organizations, etc. Usually the data from these sources/agencies is available free of cost, sometimes the library subscribes from commercial provides if demanded by users. This single platform access to users is much help for research. Following agencies/ sources are listed:

- Data Sets
- indiastat.com
- India Data Portal
- United Nations (UN) Data Portal
- International Monetary Fund (IMF) Data
- World Bank Data

Another big platform is Institutional Repository where the research output of JNU researchers is archived for wider access.

viii. Subject Gateway

The subject gateway is very helpful in locating the

information sources by the choice of subject. The features are such as users can view search Results for Resources by Title and Description, browse the JNU Collection, find Research Guides etc.

ix. Open access

The Open Access facility has become popular among students. Following kinds of resources are directed by JNU website:

- Journals
- e-Books
- Institutional Repositories
- E-Databases
- Audio E-Book
- Directory of Open Access Journals
- Taylor & Francis
- Computational Linguistics (MIT)26 (2000) TO Current
- Sankhya (from Indian Statistical Institute), from 1993 to Current; it is available in full Text and there are special Issues 2005 onwards
- Journal of Human Ecology;
- Advances in production Engineering and Management
- Journal of Social Sciences;
- Journal of Sociology and Social Anthropology;
- Mathematics Seminar;
- Articles by Nobel Prize Laureates -2012
- Public Library of Science
- Medknow Publications; these are publishing on behalf of various learned societies as well as associations.
- Indian Council of Medical Research
- ADB Review 31 (1997) Onwards

- Andhra Pradesh Monthly
- Journal of Life Sciences;
- Journal of Economics;
- The Anthropologist;
- Studies on Home and Community Science;
- Studies of Tribes and Tribals;
- Journal of Psychology;
- Journal of Intelligence and Security Issues;
- International Journal of Educational Sciences
- International Journal of Human Genetics
- Journal of History and Archaeology;
- The Journal of Biology;
- The Journal of Genetics ;
- Academic Journals (Science, Art, Education, Legal);
- Journal of Human Biology;
- Studies on Ethno-Medicine;
- AERA (Education) ;
- AgEcon (Agriculture and Applied Economics) ;
- AGRICOLA (Agriculture) ;
- Arnetminer ;
- arXiv (Physics, Math, Computer Science, Biology) ;
- ASCE (Civil Engineering) ;
- Bioline International (Health and Medicine) ;
- BioMedCentral (Biomedical, Medicine,Biology &Biotechnology) ;
- Chemistry Central (Chemistry);
- CogPrints;
- DBLP (Comp.Sc. Bibliography);
- DIRLINE (Health Information);

- DOAJ (Dirctory of Open access Journal) Multi-disciplinary;
- Educational Technology & Society;
- Electronic Journal Library;
- ERIC (Education Resources Information Centre);
- Free Medical Journals;
- HighWire (Life sciences, medicine, physical and social sciences.);
- Index Translation (Literature in translation)
- Ingentaconnect (Multi-disciplinary)
- Journal of Digital Information
- MedlinePlus (Medical science)
- Nature.com (Multi-disciplinary)
- Open J-Gate
- PubMed (Medical Science)
- SPIE (Optics and Photonics)
- Strategian (Multi disciplinary)
- The Collection of Computer science Bibliography

The above list includes various kinds of resources, platforms and websites which provide open access facilities/ resources.

x. ETD Repository

The JNU's ETD Repository is storing Theses with the aim to provide reference service to user community. The Central Library has maintained a vast and separate collection of theses and dissertation. The bibliographical details are accessible by the users through OPAC. The theses are available from the year 1960. Last year there were 21,000 theses and dissertations awarded in various subjects as humanities, social sciences & sciences disciplines. It has approximately 18,000 unique titles in this section. The library will make available "Table of Contents (TOC)" of these documents available online. Users will be able to search through OPAC. In 2012, the library started project for digitization. Till date, there are more than 17,000 hard volumes which have been digitized. The MoU with INFLIBNET Centre has guided the university to have now digitized copy of more than 5,000 PhD theses. These are available in 'Shodhganga' through INFLIBNET.

i. E-Thesis

The Jawaharlal Nehru University Library has approximately 5000 theses and dissertations in Shodhganga. The subject/center/school wise listing is as following:

- Center for Development Studies;
- Center for Historical Studies;
- enter of Educational Studies;
- Central Drug Research Institute;
- Central Institute for Medicinal and Aromatic Plants;
- Centre for Biotechnology;
- Centre for Cellular and Molecular Biology;
- Centre for Diplomacy, International Law and Economics;
- Centre for International Politics Organisation and disarmament;
- Centre for Molecular and Cellular Biology;
- Centre for Molecular Medicine;
- Centre for Political Studies;
- Centre for Sanskrit Studies;
- Centre for Social Medicine and Community Health;
- Centre for the study of Law and Governance;
- Centre of Indian Language;
- Department of Economics;

- Department of Physics;
- Department of Soil Science and Agricultural Chemistry;
- Institute of Defence Studies and Analyses;
- Institute of Microbial Technology;
- International Centre for Genetic Engineering and Biotechnology;
- National Institute of Immunology;
- National Institute of Plant Genome Research;
- Nuclear Science Centre;
- Raman Research Institute;
- School of Arts and Aesthetics;
- School of Biotechnology;
- School of Computational and Integrative Sciences;
- School of Computer and System Science;
- School of Environmental Sciences;
- School of Information Technology;
- School Of International Legal Studies;
- School of International Studies;
- School of Language Literature and Culture Studies;
- School of Life Sciences;
- School of Physical Science;
- School of Social Sciences;
- Southeast Asian and South West Pacific Studies

xii. Press Clippings

Since last five decades of academic journey, JNU Library has developed a huge archive of Press Clippings. The users find news items on Indian Politics, Social Problems, Education, Law & Criminalization and news about JNU etc. in the Database. With the help of VTLS Library Management Software, this is maintained. In the recent past the library has digitized approximately 8 lakhs newspaper articles pulled out from over 30 English newspapers from India and abroad. Apart from this, the JNU Library also subscribed following news services etc.:

- *PressDisplay* : It is an online newspaper database to complement the press clippings database. This database covers 2000 newspapers from 100 countries in 60 languages.
- *NK News* : It is a provider of primary and secondary data on North Korea that is unavailable anywhere else and research tools specifically tailored for users within government and academia.
- *ProQuest Historical Newspapers* : In this collection, there are "The Guardian" (1821-2003) and "The Observer" (1791-2003)
- *ProQuest Historical Newspapers* : To access, there "The Wall Street Journal" (1889-1996).
- Library has rare collection of Urdu newspaper "Al-Islah".

FOR INTERNATIONAL STUDENTS

Understanding and relating to international students, this is significant for a library to exercise extra efforts in order to loosen the cultural barriers in the new educational environment. Turning towards the international students, the central library is provisioning to offer services of varied nature. The quality services are the duties of libraries. The library endeavors and thoroughly acquaints the international users with the rules-regulations and resources combined with services. As the international students should use library's services, the unfamiliarity with library services may make it uncomfortable. The sizeable segment of international students requires personal assistance and sometimes more efforts within the library. To provide information services by creating a modern environment has been a complex yet simple objective of JNU library. The policies, guidelines and users' expectations have functioned as instructive techniques to fulfill users' needs. The following facets of modernity at JNU library narrate a journey taken till so far:

- Faculty members and students find the print resources and digital resources available by spending time on the library portal.
- Students spend more of their time accessing library.
- Resources: remotely or onsite at the library?
- The library website has become a face of modern library at JNU.
- Library staff helps the faculty members in their teaching responsibility by providing them resources and service timely.
- The library staff assists faculty members and students.
- Faculty members and students are given information literacy trainings by library.
- Faculty members and students utilize library resources in both the format i.e. print and digital.
- Faculty members timely find the resources which are required for academic purposes.
- Library facilities are improved when these are utilized by faculty members as there is continuous interaction and feedback.

REFERENCES

1. Barton Lessin, Rhonda McGinnis & Rick Bean. Guidelines and Standards Applicable for Library Services to Distance Education Business Programs, Journal of Business & Finance Librarianship Volume 7, Issue 2-3, January 2002, pages 155-205
2. Beth S. Woodard & Lisa Janicke Hinchliffe. Technology and Innovation in Library Instruction Management. Journal of Library AdministrationVolume 36, Issue 1-2, January 2002, pages 39-55

3. Brendan Fitzgerald, (2006) "VICNET and Victoria's virtual library: a decade of online achievements", The Electronic Library, Vol. 24 Iss: 1, pp.5 - 10
4. Chinwe Veronica Anunobi, Majesty Ignatius Ezeani, (2011) "Digital library deployment in a university: Challenges and prospects", Library Hi Tech, Vol. 29 Iss: 2, pp.373 – 386
5. Faranak Mohsenzadeh, Alireza Isfandyari Moghaddam, (2009) "Application of information technologies in academic libraries", The Electronic Library, Vol. 27 Iss: 6, pp.986 - 998
6. Faye Chadwell , Shan C. Sutton , (2014) "The future of open access and library publishing", New Library World, Vol. 115 Iss: 5/6, pp.225 - 236
7. Golnessa Galyani Moghaddam, V.G. Talawar, (2009) "Library consortia in developing countries: an overview", Program, Vol. 43 Iss: 1, pp.94 - 104
8. Harry M. Kibirige, Lisa DePalo, (2001) "The education function in a digital library environment: a challenge for college and research libraries", The Electronic Library, Vol. 19 Iss: 5, pp.283 – 295
9. http://jnuonlinecatlog.jnu.ac.in:8080/search/query;jsessionid=BB87 F121E9C8878B5A167CC55A6A3A71?theme=jnu
10. http://www.sitegeekinfotech.com/demo/jnu/
11. http://lib.jnu.ac.in/Onilne_Databases
12. Jayshree Mamtora, (2013) "Transforming library research services: towards a collaborative partnership", Library Management, Vol. 34 Iss: 4/5, pp.352 – 371
13. http://lib.jnu.ac.in/Plagiarism
14. JNU Library website. http://lib.jnu.ac.in/
15. http://lib.jnu.ac.in/Online_Journals
16. http://lib.jnu.ac.in/e-books
17. http://lib.jnu.ac.in/E-Newspapers
18. http://ezproxy.jnu.ac.in/login
19. http://www.openathens.net/
20. http://lib.jnu.ac.in/Trial_Resources
21. http://lib.jnu.ac.in/Data_Centre
22. http://lib.jnu.ac.in/Subject/subjects/ajaxsearch.php
23. http://lib.jnu.ac.in/content/jnu%E2%80%99s-etd-repository
24. http://jnuonlinecatlog.jnu.ac.in:8080/search/query?facet_item_class=39&sort=dateBookAdded&theme=jnu

25. http://lib.jnu.ac.in/Press_Clipping

26. Julian Aiken & Fred Shapiro. The Yale Law Library, On Demand: A Holistic Approach to Library Services. Legal Reference Services QuarterlyVolume 33, Issue 3, July 2014, pages 226-238

27. Julie Sibthorpe, (2009) "Libraries without Walls 7: Exploring "Anywhere, Anytime" Delivery of Library Services: Proceedings of an International Conference held on 14 18 September 2007, organised by the Centre for Research in Library and Information Management (CERLIM), Manchester Metropolitan University", Library Management, Vol. 30 Iss: 3, pp.216 - 218

28. Kristiina Hormia Poutanen, Iiris Kuusinen, Jarmo Saarti, Pentti Vattulainen, (2011) "The teaching and research environment in Finland in 2020: University and polytechnic libraries in a digital service network", Library Management, Vol. 32 Iss: 8/9, pp.599 - 611

29. Peter Moloney. Kogarah Municipal Library: library automation and innovation diffusion—a study. The Australian Library JournalVolume 46, Issue 2, January 1997, pages 154-160

30. Robin Frederick Guy, (2000) "Developing the hybrid library: progress to date in the National Library of Scotland", The Electronic Library, Vol. 18 Iss: 1, pp.40 - 50

31. Simon Francis, (2002) "Implementing the VTLS library management system at Tomsk State University Library: impact on management", Program, Vol. 36 Iss: 3, pp.166 - 175

32. Thoah Kim Thi Ninh, Kerry Tanner, Graeme Johanson, Tom Denison, (2010) "Systematic performance measurement for university libraries in Vietnam", Library Management, Vol. 31 Iss: 8/9, pp.702 - 716

33. Tracy Primich & Caroline Richardson. The Integrated Library System. The Acquisitions Librarian, Volume 18, Issue 35-36, September 2005, pages 119-133

34. Wang Baoji, Zhu Jinnuo, Xu Ruiqing, Luo Qingsheng & Liu Qingshui. Innovation in agricultural digital library services based on Web 2.0. New Zealand Journal of Agricultural Research, Volume 50, Issue 5, December 2007, pages 1255-1260

35. Yared Mammo. Haramaya University Library and Information Services: Looking back to look forward. The International Information & Library ReviewVolume 42, Issue 1, March 2010, pages 14-2

7

Restoring and Building for Future

How the old services, infrastructures were repaired and taken into consideration for future planning, also transitions. Major visible changes due to changed academic, organizational and social environments.

INTRODUCTION

The library is imagined and supposed to be a calm and comfortable place where the readers can read quietly. The users may differ in the assumption of a library becoming a tranquil place or a place for interaction. The simple 'printed books only' environment or the highly sophisticated 'computerized' ambience may be two choices for library users in top priority at the same time. The kinds of customer gratification with a motive to please the user are found pervasive in this highly Internet-charged environment, the libraries are expected to serve in the same 'click and get it' manner. The information products and services have become web-based entities to be served before the library users regardless of the efforts made by the libraries to reach at this stage. The advancement in the web-technologies and users' expectations, there are myriad challenges before the libraries.

The challenges are in the form and shape of:

a. Understanding the user expectations

b. Creating the interfaces to know and exploit user feedback

c. Relating to user expectations

While concentrating on the users' expectations, the needle moves towards the needs and wants of the library users. There are chances when the new entrants and old readers may both require the assistance to navigate through the library building and resources. The understanding of level of skills possessed by both kinds of library readers plays a significant role to frame their expectations into the services. The guided tours into the knowledge corridors or the undefined tracks both can be helpful for the readers given they reach to right resource. The trust develops when the readers receive the services they expect. The JNU Central library has created the trust between readers and library's navigations. The beginning of academic session takes place by developing a relation with the library users. The supportive team of the library advises the students about how to use the library's resources and services. The anxiety of the students is the target of library team to strike and remove.

The common scenario at academic libraries at the beginning of new session is that the students are unaware of the full range of library services and resources and they need to be helped by the library. At JNU library, the collaboration between librarian and faculty are in such a way that leads towards the greater use of library by the students. To enhance the awareness and usage of e-resources, the library comes out with new methods and opportunities.

LIBRARY SERVICES AND EXPECTATIONS

Keeping the users' demand and needs in mind, the library designed its services which match the academic goals of the library users. Due to impressive planning and implementation, the library has become more user-centered. Being a responsible institution in tandem with organizational objectives, JNU library recreated the library services; the services more useful due to their technology based deliverance. The methods, mechanisms and deliverables are melting the ice and meeting the needs and users' expectations. The journey on the basis of high principles of librarianship takes place on the perceptions made by library's achievements. The library focused on the customers' characteristics, factors of motivations and the targeted outcomes. The library in itself is a complex system yet to inherit the understanding of user perceptions. The customer based assessments have played a role in planning and implementation of the recreated services.

WHY INNOVATE AND RECREATE?

The innovation and recreation of the library services have been based on adopting modern methods and tools. The library does not hesitate in using the modern, popular gadgets and equipments with the purpose to increase in efficiency as well as effectiveness. Definitely the speed and enthusiasm of the part of library is also visible. So inevitable it was to have included computer applications in library services, to enhance timely and interactive services. The application of open source software and techniques has brought the decrease in cost and delays. JNU library is among those few libraries which are at the matured state of computerization, web based library services, remote services to the thousands of users. The operational and functional aspects display the appropriateness of methods applied. The reasons behind this may be categorized as:

i. Innovation

ii. Productivity

It is achieved by the successful formation of individual/group capabilities through motivation support, resources support and information support. The method to renovate the existing services usually follows a need to visualize the desired outcomes and the path of increased incorporation of web applications. Certainly the well planned strategy supports the library vision and the quality of services. The emphasis has been on the identification of gaps which existed previously and bridging the same. The use of State-of-the-art information technology has been taken into consideration to implement in library services. The demand of services keeping the technologies in vogue is not something undesirable by students or faculty members. The aspirations to have a world-class library begin with the library services as exist in few highly modernized libraries around the globe.

The discussions during Library Advisory Committee Meetings, informal talks and the casual chats with the students, the librarian finds the core of their needs and pragmatic suggestions as well. In this context, it is appropriate to mention the rightly placed 'suggestion box' so that people concerned with the library can be interactive with the librarian. Though the interface is already and always established through the ways of e-mails, telephonic conversations etc. yet this beautiful small box provides another opportunity to be face to face with librarian.

The entire exercise is towards creating faith and confidence in the library; the users have for their service. The innovative and modern library services go through the phases of initiation and evaluation with the mobilization of information technology. Entire procedure is continuous with the constant eye on the goals earlier decided. It has always kept in mind during the last few years to maintain the relation between the information technology and goals of library. The component factors are as:

i. Chosen and implemented technology contextual with JNU academic goals.

ii. The capability of information technology to accomplish the goals and meet the users' expectations.

The input of innovation and new technologies in library services began with logical extension in the previously existing services, without distorting the framed the library system.

Leading from the paternalistic ways to self-supporting mechanism has been the goal of JNU library. Creation of new website of library, sustaining the newly implemented services without any outside source are few examples where library has shown the self-supporting approach. Cost-benefit analysis is taken into account to make the continuous growth possible. The library has endeavored to apply the 'Technology Transfer' to induce the full potential of IT in the library services. The self-reliance approach has been put into action while collection building, developing services and disseminating the information. In creating the self-reliant and self-supporting system, the library has considered the value of proper utilization of its resources. Thus the *integration of various approaches* has placed the library among the highly influential organization.

To meet the users' expectations in terms of innovative and demand oriented services, the library has considered following aspects such as:

i. Understanding the demands and sustaining the commitment

ii. Involvement of related experts to up bring the services

iii. Maintaining the cooperation as well as coordination in each target oriented library service

iv. Taking services of ad-hoc task personnel

MAJOR GUIDELINES AND GUIDING FORCES

Every organization has goals, objectives and achievements which are guided by the strong professional intuition as well as day-today sense of convenience. The JNU library has taken the highly sophisticated tasks and simple steps to meet the user expectations. The emphasis has been on the following:

i. Converting the library into a place of learning as well as interaction
ii. The provision of library services round the clock and round the year
iii. Understanding users' needs or demands and expectations
iv. Provision of customized facilities
v. Increasing efficiency and targets

REFERENCE SERVICE

The library planned to make provisions for rendering the services in more interactive way to the library readers. The presence of vast collections of print and electronic format documents needs to have those methods to reach to users which are easy, suitable and promising to bring out the relevant information. The designing of reference service was planned to be an interface of the library.

The library staff is trained specially for the reference services because the number of student is very large compared to other universities. It has not been an easy task to provide reference service to a vast number of users belonging to a diverse subject fields. The way the user puts his or her query may not be uniform and this situation always puzzles the library staff how to satisfy the information demand of the user. Few simple aspects such as assistance for general enquiries, guidance regarding the organization of the Library and use of the WEBOPAC are always visible in the reference section. The "MAY I HELP YOU" desk to assist users on each floor is a kind of feature that is not found in general.

NEW ARRIVALS

The library acquires the reading material for the users and it is the duty of library to inform the readers about the acquisition of documents. The announcement of new arrivals is significant for the readers who requested it, also for those who have general interest. The users are informed by the running banner of new arrivals on the library website as well as personalized email services. During the intimation of the new arrivals, the new books are placed on display for one week for all the users for reference. After this time frame, the book is issued to the user who has recommended for procurement.

TECHNOLOGY SPACES

The technology spaces are very much in the demand in the JNU Central Library. These spaces provide a complete freedom to the users for using the technology facilities in the form of wifi facility and e-resources. To specify here, the 'Cyberlibrary' is located near the main entrance of library at the ground floor. A big number of computers (approx. 200) are installed with linux for the use of Students/Research Scholars and Faculty Members. This technology space 'Cyberlibrary' is meant to facilitate the access to the kinds of e-resources of library. These e-resources include online subscribed resources of the library, Digitized theses and dissertations, digital newspaper clippings. This featured service of library supports users to write their article, term paper, theses or dissertations from this area. The computers are well equipped with Internet facility where users can access it with the authorized inter-net access ID. The guest users are provided the temporary Internet access ID on request.

HELEN KELLER UNIT

The academic libraries have been striving to reach the visually challenged students also. The journey began with the understanding of their information needs and identification of means to provide them the desired information. The physical accessibility to the visually impaired students is a significant aspect to be considered in terms of library's vision towards the blind and low vision students. To design an efficient service by the library, there have been few factors such as:

i. The information needs of visually challenged/impaired students.

ii. How the information needs can be fulfilled?

iii. The problems faced by students as well as library.

The information needs of the visually impaired students are related with:

i. daily living and studies

ii. the visual disabilities and health related concepts

iii. financial, government information

iv. reading, recreation, and travel etc.

The information needs reflect about the choice which seems similar to the choice and need of other students of library. Apart from the library, the informal sources such as friends, family members and other social groups provide them the information. Looking into the past practices of libraries, it is found that libraries were serving the visually challenged people by providing them specific books such as talking books. By the advent of Adaptive technology, the situations tend to progress. In the mean time, the JNU library also sought support from other organizations to serve the visually impaired students. To popularize the use of library among the visually impaired students, it created awareness programs and distributed computer equipments also. The discomfort felt by such students was brought to minimum so that they can easily express and find their information needs. The library paid attention to their information requirements, the physical limitations and also to the methods to serve them. To provide effective services, the crucial component has been the presence of trained staff. Trained staffs are working to serve the visually impaired students. Library staff should be accessible and supporting to these students.

The provision of continuous services is the ongoing project with a goal to facilitate the information services to visually-challenged people at the JNU campus. There is entire team working for visually-impaired students to provide the support of adaptive technology. Also these students are welcomed to suggest and inform about their information based requirements and to improve the infrastructure, methods to provide services etc. Such components build a better system. The demonstrated view of equipments and documents develops the curiosity as well as enhances the usage power. During the trainings, demonstrations and provision of services the library staff interacts directly with the visually impaired students. The awareness and sensitivity level of library staff towards this kind of students' group always play a great role.

The growth of number of students during these couple of years has been cause and concern of developments in number of assistance and equipments for the visually challenged students. The use of assistive and adaptive technology has been a boon for their learning. The assistance may initiate with the simple reading to advanced web searches. The one of its kind of service is the service meant for visually challenged students. The Central Library is providing special service to the visually challenged students and researchers of the University. An entire section named 'Helen Keller Unit' is meant for the visually challenged students etc. This service is being provided by using advanced assistive technologies.

The Helen Keller unit is equipped with 30 computers, each installed with JAWS (screen reading software), Kurzweil 1000 (OCR software) and computer headphones. In addition, to these 20 HP flatbed scanners, 02 Lexcam scanners, 02 Braille refreshable display and 02 Braille embossers are also provided. The software installed in the computers of this unit supports different European and Hindi Language. The library did not stop here itself but extended the services to different School/Centres like SSS-I, SSS-II, SIS, CSLG and Sanskrit Centre. Moreover to extension, the library has also distributed 52 Angle Daisy Player (Digital Voice recorder) to each student to record their classroom lectures. Library has distributed 40 Dell make Laptops to M. Phil and Ph. D scholars.

To support more number of visually challenged students, the library has provided the locker facilities up to M. Phil. and Ph. D scholars, visually challenged and also to the physical Handicapped students/researchers. 15 Wheelchairs were provided by EOO for the Physically Challenged students to be distributed by the Central Library. Apart from this, 5 computers are provided (reserved) at ground floor of the Library for the physically challenged students.

In addition to the previously mentioned facilities for the visually challenged students, the library has subscribed to bookshare.org. This subscription is meant to facilitate and provide the relevant collection in different formats such as daisy, mp3 and e-text. By becoming member of Daisy Forum of India (DFI), the library has planned to support in research activities at greater level. Library organizes training and orientation programme on the uses of assistive technology for the benefit of these students so that they can make use of the latest assistive technologies in their day to day studies.

REPROGRAPHY SERVICE

For the reprographic services, the students' requirements and satisfaction are always important considerations for a library in context with number of machines deployed. The JNU library provides quality based photocopying services to library users. The initiation of strong photocopying and imaging service is significant when talked about the users' services. Depending upon needs of library users, the reprographic and scanning facilities are maintained. The photocopy facility is offered to students against payment. The scanning services were initiated keeping the needs and demands of students in mind. The scanning facility is provided to the visually challenged students of the University.

INTERLIBRARY LOANS

Inter Library Loan (ILL) service is important in the age of shrinking budgets and growing information demands of the students. On a regular basis, the ILL supports the readers' services. Through ILL, library serves a big number of users' requests. The ILL is very useful and becoming an assistance to readers in JNU library. Except very few libraries in the world which are capable of providing any title to the reader which is demanded. The concept and service of Inter Library Loan (ILL) has proven very helpful to the readers in the JNU Central Library. The ILL has been helpful to arrange books and other reading materials for the students. The students are encouraged to send their request by e-mail and written applications also. While conversing about the various services of library, the role of Information Desk cannot be ignored. The Information Desk provides a single platform for all types of queries from the users.

The location also plays a great role in offering the services to readers and even to non-readers. It is located on the ground floor near the entrance. Various small yet intense services it provides such as directional assistance on site and over the telephone. It facilitates the referral service for readers with queries beyond the directional purposes or holdings verification stage to the Inter Library Loan desk or service points. This Information Desk serves for the queries about services, accessing electronic resources and technology in the Library.

Though the library is working round the clock yet to serve the readers from far too, there is the facility of downloading various kinds of forms and information such as:

- Membership form for Students (Hindi)
- Membership form for Guest Faculty/Special Members(Hindi)
- Library Clearance form for Students (Hindi)
- Library Clearance form for Faculty/Staff (Hindi)
- Library Consultation Form (Hindi)
- Library Rules (Hindi)

SERVICES TO AVOID PLAGIARISM

The library website helps in creating awareness among students regarding what is plagiarism and how to avoid it. To create awareness among the students and other academic users, the Central Library has designed a program of specific activities. Library organizes lectures, workshops and other programs to initiate the sense of avoiding plagiarism and how to contribute an original good research. There have been a number of awareness and training programs to sustain the originality in research. The overwhelming response from the student and other members of academic community has motivated the library to conduct such informative programs and workshops.

MAKING THE SERVICES REACH TO ENTIRE ORGANIZATION

The creation of library web portal and listing the various services do not amount to fulfillment of goals of libraries. The planning and implementation to reach to each student of JNU has been one of the objectives of library. To inform and provide the services to the maximum number of students, the library keep on visiting the centers, schools by arranging workshops, training programs. With the active collaboration of faculty members, the library has been able to coordinate such activities. The library is constantly conscious to design and implement any library service keeping in view the needs, expectations and demands of students. Each complaint and suggestion functions as opportunity for the library to understand the students closely. Surely, this works to improve the service; and the improvements in users' services a continuous process which is fueled by patience and right implementation.

REFERENCES

1. Al Harrasi Nabhan, Hassan Jabur Naeema, (2014) "Factors contributing to successful collaboration among Omani academic libraries", Interlending & Document Supply, Vol. 42 Iss: 1, pp.26 - 32
2. Ahmed Taha, (2012) "Networked library services in a research intensive university", The Electronic Library, Vol. 30 Iss: 6, pp.844 - 856
3. Andrew C. White, (2002) "Using heterogeneous components to construct online library portals", The Electronic Library, Vol. 20 Iss: 3, pp.224 – 230
4. Anna Koulikourdi, (2008) "Assistive technologies in Greek libraries", Library Hi Tech, Vol. 26 Iss: 3, pp.387 - 397
5. Briony Train, Pete Dalton, Judith Elkin, (2000) "Embracing inclusion: the critical role of the library", Library Management, Vol. 21 Iss: 9, pp.483 - 491
6. Buhle Mbambo Thata, (2010) "Assessing the impact of new technology on internal operations: With special reference to the

introduction of mobile phone services at UNISA Library", Library Management, Vol. 31 Iss: 6, pp.466 - 475

7. Colleen S. Harris, (2011) "Delegation at the macro level: library IT, spheres of influence, and the promise of cloudware", The Bottom Line, Vol. 24 Iss: 1, pp.55 – 57
8. Dalling John , Rafferty Pauline , (2013) "Open source, open minds?: An investigation into attitudes towards open source library management systems in UK higher education libraries", Program: electronic library and information systems, Vol. 47 Iss: 4, pp.399 - 423
9. Helen M. Byamugisha, (2010) "Digitizing library resources for new modes of information use in Uganda", Library Management, Vol. 31 Iss: 1/2, pp.42 - 56
10. http://jnuonlinecatlog.jnu.ac.in:8080/search/query;jsessionid=BB87F121E9C8878B5A167CC55A6A3A71?theme=jnu
11. http://www.sitegeekinfotech.com/demo/jnu/
12. http://lib.jnu.ac.in/Onilne_Databases
13. Jayshree Mamtora, (2013) "Transforming library research services: towards a collaborative partnership", Library Management, Vol. 34 Iss: 4/5, pp.352 - 371
14. JNU Library website. http://lib.jnu.ac.in/
15. http://lib.jnu.ac.in/Online_Journals
16. http://lib.jnu.ac.in/Download
17. http://lib.jnu.ac.in/e-books
18. http://lib.jnu.ac.in/E-Newspapers
19. http://ezproxy.jnu.ac.in/login
20. http://www.openathens.net/
21. http://lib.jnu.ac.in/Trial_Resources
22. http://lib.jnu.ac.in/Data_Centre
23. http://lib.jnu.ac.in/Subject/subjects/ajaxsearch.php
24. http://lib.jnu.ac.in/content/jnu%E2%80%99s-etd-repository
25. http://jnuonlinecatlog.jnu.ac.in:8080/search/query?facet_item_class=39&sort=dateBookAdded&theme=jnu
26. http://lib.jnu.ac.in/Press_Clipping
27. http://lib.jnu.ac.in/information-vh-students
28. I.V. Malhan, (2006) "Developing corporate culture in the Indian university libraries: Problems and challenges of change management", Library Management, Vol. 27 Iss: 6/7, pp.486 - 493

29. Jacqueline Chelin, (1999) "Facilitating access to one and all: report of a project carried out at UWE, Bristol to facilitate access to learning resources for students and staff with disabilities", Library Review, Vol. 48 Iss: 6, pp.283 – 290

30. JNU Library website. http://lib.jnu.ac.in/

31. Mark Stover, (2000) "Technological concerns for library managers", Library Management, Vol. 21 Iss: 9, pp.472 - 483

32. Lew Sook-Ling , Maizatul Akmar Ismail , Yuen Yee-Yen , (2015) "Information infrastructure capability and organisational competitive advantage: Framework", International Journal of Operations & Production Management, Vol. 35 Iss: 7, pp.1032 - 1055

33. Marion Beaton, (2005) "Glasgow City Council: library, information and learning services for disabled people in Glasgow", Library Review, Vol. 54 Iss: 8, pp.472 - 478

34. Mel Collier, (2006) "Strategic change in higher education libraries with the advent of the digital library during the fourth decade of *Program*", Program, Vol. 40 Iss: 4, pp.334 - 345

35. Ohene Sakyi Awuku, (1995) "Productivity in university libraries of developing countries: a West and Southern African perspective", Library Management, Vol. 16 Iss: 3, pp.24 - 33

36. Robert Newton, Audrey Sutton, Mike McConnell, (1998) "Information skills for open learning: a public library initiative", Library Review, Vol. 47 Iss: 2, pp.125 – 134

37. Sally Wilson, Graham McCarthy, (2010) "The mobile university: from the library to the campus", Reference Services Review, Vol. 38 Iss: 2, pp.214 - 232

38. Shabahat Husain , Mohammad Nazim , (2015) "Use of different information and communication technologies in Indian academic libraries", Library Review, Vol. 64 Iss: 1/2, pp.135 - 153

39. Stephen Cramond, (1999) "Efforts to formalise international collaboration in scholarly information infrastructure", Library Hi Tech, Vol. 17 Iss: 3, pp.272 - 282

40. Terry Cottrell, (2013) "Good libraries are expensive libraries?", The Bottom Line, Vol. 26 Iss: 2, pp.47 – 51

41. Tom Wilding, (2002) "External partnerships and academic libraries", Library Management, Vol. 23 Iss: 4/5, pp.199 – 202.

8

Community Building and Library

Endeavors and Role of Library In past 3 years
Various simple, informal ways taken to serve the academic community

INTRODUCTION

Community building involves a lot of efforts and well planned implementations. The JNU library has been able to design those kinds of programs that make it outreach to the academic community it is meant to serve, thus building its own place in community. The endeavors by the JNU library can be identified as training programs, lectures, workshops etc. These are encapsulated and described measuring as:

a. Training Program

The training programs by the JNU library have always been popular leading to full rooms leaving no space for lack of enthusiasm among the students. The following table displays information about the topics, timings and trainings conducted by library in nut shell.

Table 1

Training Programme
Training Program on SciFinder for Academic Research
Orientation cum-Training Programme on "URKUND Plagiarism detection tool provided by INFLIBNET"
Training/Orientation Program on Assistive Technologies for Visually Challenged Research Scholars & Students
Central Library is going to organize Orientation Program on Library Resources and Research Support Services : SSS &SAA , SIS & SCL&G , SLL&CS & SCSS and All Science Schools
Orientation program on Library E-Resources and Services
Discovery services a demonstration-cum-orientation
How to use EBSCO E-Books Library
Hands on Training and Practices for offering Library Services
Assistive Technologies for Visually Challenged Research Scholars & Students
Orientation program on Library E-Resources and Services
Creation of JNU ETD Archive using DSpacece
User Education-cum-orientation Programme on DIGITAL RESOURCES
Training of Master Trainers in use of ASSISTIVE TECHNOLOGIES
USER EDUCATION-CUM-ORIENTATION Programme on DIGITAL RESOURCES
Presentation and Demonstration Program on EDS (EBSCO Discovery Service) for providing single window access to all E-resources of JNU Library

(***Source:*** JNU Library Website. http://lib.jnu.ac.in/)

Various community building programs are given as following:

i. Single Window Access Demonstration Program

The EDS ("EBSCO Discovery Service") is meant for having search facility through "single window access" for the entire collection of Library, JNU.

Central Library, JNU endeavored in the direction of facilitating users to access entire collection at one click. Instead of roaming or browsing the various kinds of sources one by one, this facility is a wonder for users. Central Library organized a comprehensive program to make users comfortable with this facility; they were trained about its features and how to access it. The presentation concentrated about the EBSCO Discovery Service (EDS) and its need for JNU. The other aspects covered have been:

- Discovery Vs Federated search
- Full Integration of catalogue and IR systems
- Enhancement of Catalogue
- Multi Language support features
- vMobile, Tablet access and compatibility
- Remote access system compatibility (Athens and Ezproxy)

ii. User Education-Cum-Orientation Programme On Digital Resources

The "user education-cum-orientation programme on digital resources" was conducted at Central Lirbary from 21st -24th August, 2012. The user education program has been comprehensive. It covered various databases such as LEXIS-NEXIS-Legal Database, and EBSCO All databases. These databases include Academic Search Primer, and Research databases & Econ Lit. There have been more of them as; "CMIE Databases, CEIC Databases, India Stat, Manupatra, INDLAW, Hein Online, and SIAM". The inclusion of "Science databases", "ACM Portal & IEE Explorer", and "JCCC" has paved way for users' satisfaction. The other databases such as Elsevier Science Direct and Scopus are supporting the research at large scale. The availability of Databases, Dissertation and Theses, Research support from "ProQuest" has been in these resources.

iii. Training programs related to Assistive Technologies

During this training, the participants were JNU Library Staff and Visually Challenged Students. The highly sophisticated training programs include various aspects such as:

- Common utility applications for "Basic Desktop".
- File Management system and Familiarization with ORCA to the users and trainers.
- Facilities such as Word processing Open Office word.
- Informing about the Internet Browser, Website, and Search Engines to the users and trainers. It is significant for the "Reading Web pages". There are facilities as quick search. They were also trained for doing E-mail etc.
- The training sessions included "Practical Lab" sessions also. These labs were for facilitating e-mail activity and chatting activity.
- Without training about "Multimedia", this could not have been complete. For example, activities such as "Sound and Video Menu", is necessary on the part of users. They were also told about "CD Writing" (Brasero Disc Burner). The training about USB Storage Devices has also taken place. Further training for Installation of Linux was also given.
- The trainers were trained for "Open Source Application" also.
- A "Session for the staff" was mandatory for future requirements.

iv. Creation of JNU ETD Archive using DSpace

During the first quarter of 2013, a training program on ETD creation was organized. This program was meant especially for the library staff.

v. Orientation program

A comprehensive learning session on "Library E-Resources and Services" was organized on beginning of new session in August 2013. These orientation programs have been supportive to new entrants to the JNU library system.

vi. Training / Practices for Library Services

There has been "hands on" training for how to offer various kinds of library services during the last week of year 2014 to beginning of year 2014.

vii. How to use EBSCO E-Books Library

To make the readers more acquainted with e-books, especially the use of EBSCO E-Books, the library organized many training sessions.

viii. Discovery services: a demonstration-cum-orientation

The Discovery services at the JNU library have been a great tool to access the knowledge resources at JNU. The training session on how to make best use of Discovery services was organized in the mid of 2014.

ix. Orientation program

The user orientation plays a great role in enhancing users to use the library in most powerful manner. The orientation program in the year 2014 has been as following facets of learning management:

- Central Library Resources and Services
- Plagiarisms avoidance/similarity check software Turnitin and iThenticate
- EBSCO Discovery Services
- EBSCO Research Databases &EBSCO E-books
- Economic Intelligence Unit- Country Reports
- Indian Citation Index

- News Paper Direct and Times of India Archive
- Summon Web Scale Discovery Service, Proquest Academic Research Library, DNSA, Proquest Dissertation and Thesis & Literature Online with MLA
- Presentation on Journal Citation Report & Indlaw
- Presentation on Manupatra Presentation on Emerald E-Journals Presentation on IndiaStat.com Presentation on CEIC Macroeconomic Database (Asia)
- Presentation on Prowess & Economic Outlook
- Presentation on World Bank E-library
- Presentation on Science Online etc.
- Presentation on Web of Science & End Note
- Presentation on IEEE Xplore and ACM
- Presentation on Science Direct, Scifinder, Scopus
- Presentation on Mendeley
- Presentation on Wiley Inter Science, Wiley Protocols
- Nature Journals
- Presentation on South Asia Archive & Taylor and Francis E-Journals
- Cambridge E-Books & E-journals Collection
- Oxford E-books & E-journals Collection
- Springer E-books, E-Journals Collection & Lecture Notes in Computer Science (LNCS)
- JCCC
- MathSciNet
- Sage E-Journals and HSS Package

INVOLVING PEOPLE: BOOK RELEASE ACTIVITIES

The library has found another innovative method to connect with academic community by providing them a platform for the Book Release programs and academic discourses. The following table displays various such programs taken place time to time in the library and outside:

Table 2

Title
Central Library JNU, welcomes you to the Launch of the Book function of "Medical Insurance Scheme for the poor" by Prof.S.K. Sopory, Vice-Chancellor, JNU
Central Library, JNU welcomes you to the Book Discussion on "RAJKAMAL CHOUDHARY RACHANAWALI" Date :17/09/2015 Time:4:30 PM at Committee Room, Central Library
Central Library JNU, welcomes you to the Book Release function of "Diaspora, Culture and Identity" by Prof. Poonam Bala and launch by General Dr. V.K. Singh, Minister of State for Overseas Indian Affairs and Prof. Sudha Pai, Rector-I, JNU
Meet the Author of "Mandate:Will of the People" Dr. Vir Sanghvi on 7th May 2015
आदिवासी साहित्य के दूसरे अंक का लोकार्पण एवं परिचर्चा
Book Release function of "The Weight of Violence:Religion, Language, Politics" on 11th March 2015
Labyrinths of Language: Philosophical and Cultural Investigations
Pioneers of Library Movement in India
KRANTIVEER BHAGAT SINGH: Abhyuodey aur Bhavishya
Book Talk and Panel Discussion based on title "Hashiye ka Vratant"
Japanese Language Education : A Bridge between LANGUAGE & CULTURE

(***Source:*** JNU Library Website. http://lib.jnu.ac.in/)

LECTURES: INITIATIVE TO SPREAD LEARNING INNOVATIVELY

The way this library has invented a relationship with its academic community is paving way to explore the means to connect with readers. The lecture series has been held continuously and regularly to make learning independent of classroom and more involvement of discussions. The lectures have been helpful in discovering the other areas of same academic fields. The variety of exposures supports the learning by different sources. The details in a concise manner are presented in the table given as:

LECTURE SERIES

Table 3

Topics	*Date*
"World Bank"	
"Plagiarism"	
"How to get it published in Academic Journals"	15 March 2015
"Addressing Inequality in South Asia"	26 February 2015
"Libraries and Development: On the Agenda"	12 January 2015
Information/digital literacy initiatives	5 January 2015
North Carolina State University Libraries: Trends and Challenges"	15 October 2014
Open Scholarship and Higher Education Institutions	29 July 2014
Expanding Inner Horizons!	18 March 2014
Developments at the UK Open University Library	7 February 2014
Library Science and Librarianship in Swaziland	5 February 2014
Rock your paper	31 January 2014
Common heritage	23 January 2014
Multimedia Digital Library Collections	29 November 2013
Quality Assessment-Open Access	6 November 2013
Online Search Strategies for Research Scholars	4 October 2013
Social media initiatives in a University Library	11 September 2013
Building a "Print Fanzine Collection"	27 August 2013
Databib	19 March 2013
Laptop Distribution for Visually Impaired Research Scholars of JNU	4 March 2013
International Outreach in an Academic Library	11 February 2013
Knowledge Management in Academic Libraries	13 August 2012

(***Source:*** JNU Library Website. http://lib.jnu.ac.in/)

LECTURE SERIES

Table 4

Topics
Archives and Histories
Socio-economic Value through Open Public Data
E-books
Embedded Librarianship
Documentation of Oral History

(***Source:*** JNU Library Website. http://lib.jnu.ac.in/)

The refreshment of learning is another way to reach to user community and engaging the library staff. The borders melted when the speakers from outside India were present to deliver lectures, time to time. The topics covered in the lecture series have been very diverse yet limited to the universe of knowledge. The lecture on "Knowledge Management in Academic Libraries" has been reflecting the perspectives from South Africa. The subject of Oral History brought before the people by a lecture "Documentation of Oral History" has provided glimpses of experiences about the South Asian Oral History project running at the University of Washington Libraries. This topic was capable to bring the knowledge about "South Asian Oral History project" at the University of Washington which captured the history of South Asian Immigrants to Pacific Northwest.

The librarianship is not simply about the collection and dissemination of information resources, the lecture on "Embedded Librarianship" has opened innovative ways of collaboration with Faculty, displayed the growing need and methods to build academic roles of libraries. "E-books: Choices and Challenges" presented the scenario how this generation of libraries moving ahead but with a cautious pace. There has always been a need to understand the variegated needs of library readers. The covered lecture "Creating Socio-economic Value" through "Open Public

Data" reflected the presence of new technologies and doors for library techniques.

The innovative thinking encourages various kinds of public participation and engagement. It leads to ultimate use of data produced by various government agencies. The Future of the Internet Economy evolves due to the need to collaborate and work with different sectors to promote as well as expand access to public sector information. This will help in understanding the concept of "re-use" of data. The kind of information such as meteorological data, and socio-economic data, along with health and statistical data, is considered as the "raw material". This raw material requires refinement. Definitely many countries are compelled to update or modify the public information laws. In this way, the awareness for Public Sector Information (PSI) issues, technological questions varies from country to country. This requires more exercise in using data.

Such knowledge sessions show current trends in "public information" in India and inform the readers at JNU. Whereas the topics and concerns of modern economy related to information have been taken for learning, the lectures on 'Depleting Archives and Disintegrating Histories' encompass the inherent needs of libraries. The lecture has been able to provide information on the "weaknesses in the Public Record Act". It brought out to the surface about the deep crisis the Indian archives have been facing and also a need to preserve the legacy of India in context with documents. The concept of outreach has been ancient if the old practices are considered and evaluated thoroughly. The library outreach has been in the slow pace but there has been a curious approach to reach to the variety of users in recent years. "Keeping it Glocal" has provided few best practices for outreach, was the lecture which explored various facets of library outreach. Since JNU has the international reader community too, so the experiences of a librarian were shared to picture a practical advice to international scholars and students who have diversity in background and culture.

While moving towards the learning the new ways to keep with the international standards in library keeping activities, lecture on 'Databib: Cataloging the World's Data Repositories' provided sufficient information to look in that area also. The Databib (http://databib.org) is a "curated and global catalog" of research related information repositories. With the support of big number of library and information professionals more than 500 data repositories have been identified. This facilitates easy searching and accessibility for users. It has interoperability with a number of other platforms. It helps to deposit the data at one hand and on another; by providing a tool for identifying datasets, the users support their learning needs. The introduction of new section and service in a library also require receiving some experiences from other places. The lecture on "Building a Print Fanzine Collection in a Digital Era" was supportive to help enthusiastic library staff.

Again the concept of interaction and interfaces emerge before the library and the audience. The "Launching chat reference, Facebook, Twitter & other social media initiatives in a University Library" has been an interactive learning session for the library staff. This does not pause here and leads to understanding the "Art and Science" of search strategies for Research Scholars" keeping both print and online sources of information.

The need of required skills and approach has been depending upon availability of technologies so the search strategies, and search tools as discussed. The understanding of quality of sources and services in a library demands constant consideration. The recent concepts and platforms such as open access also find way into library. The lecture on "Quality Assessment and Open Access at the Faculty of Fine, Applied and Performing Arts, University of Gothenburg,

Sweden", "North Carolina State University Libraries: Trends and Challenges", "Information/digital literacy initiatives at Rice-Aron Library at Marlboro College, USA and JNU Library" and "Libraries and Development: On the Agenda", have been a deliberation towards understanding the knowledge.

The open access, the new cataloguing techniques are related with the modern libraries and so the multimedia digital libraries are popular among the users. The lecture on "Large-Scale Multimedia Digital Library Collections" has identified the problems and few challenges, which has been a step towards learning of facets such as "image acquisition and storage". Such learning sessions inform about the method of effective and efficient systems. But there is a need to keep basic aspects of communication in mind i.e. the language and the lexical elements. "Common heritage of Indian and Turkic people, lexical elements" lecture has been an effort to understand the impact of language in each sphere of life. Since the open access has been offering itself as a free immediate online platform for the research showcase, the scholars have become conscious to understand the attributes of the same. An approach of library emerged with the organization of 'Rock your paper: An open access repository', and "Enabling Open Scholarship: Open Access Policies, Issues and Resources for Higher Education Institutions" lectures which have been motivating for the library readers. Apart from the publishing methods and platforms in vogue, the open access means the "scientific research" making available to anyone and anywhere in the world. Again the learning revolves the interaction with students with the idea of informing them about the open access publishing. These movements are pervasive in the entire world; the librarianship may differ in few contexts keeping in view the local needs. A lecture on "Library Science and Librarianship in Swaziland" gave an overview about the far places. Certainly the "Library science is an interdisciplinary field" which includes the conventional practices in the varied perspectives with the help of "tools of management, information technology". During the last two centuries, the libraries have emerged as centers for learning besides the information centers.

Other lectures such as "Developments at the UK Open University Library" and 'Expanding Inner Horizons' seem reflecting the diverse areas to explore as an academic user and library staff. In the information scenario sometimes the non-governmental or civil society organizations also work to create change in the way that information is accessed, disseminated, and used throughout the world. The talk has been about the development framework and Millennium Development Goals promulgated by the United Nations. In the spread path of learning, the lecture on "World Bank" and "Knowledge sharing session on Plagiarism" followed by "How to get it published in Academic Journals" have been an informative and useful learning sessions for the reader community, specially the researchers.

WORKSHOPS

The workshops tend to inform the patron in a closer way. The following table displays the various workshops held during last couple of years.

Table 5

Topics
Plagiarism; how to publish in Academic Journals
Workshop on Plagiarism and Reference Management
Digitization Project Management and Digital Archiving
Workshop on "Book Care, Repair and Restoration"
Plagiarism and Reference Management using Mendeley
Workshop on: "SWATCHHA BHARAT ABHIYAN"
JNU in collaboration with Elsevier is organising Mendeley Workshop

Data Curation
How to Write and Get Published
Capacity Building related to Digitization
Emerald Group Publishing
Wiley Author Workshop
Elsevier Science Author Workshop
How to Write and Get Published
Institutional Repository using DSpace

(***Source :*** JNU Library Website. http://lib.jnu.ac.in/)

The Workshop on "Development of Institutional Repository using DSpace with special reference to creation of ETD Archive" aimed to create learning among library professionals on DSpace. It aimed to bridging the gap among library professionals and making them comfortable with the digital library creation, open sources software as well as open access. The direction of librarianship is revolving around the open sources and open access, this program helped in understanding these concepts and out them into practice. Certainly the knowledge gained would be supportive in creation of more number of institutional repositories. The workshop on "How to Write for and Get Published in Scientific Journals"' was related with the idea to inform researchers for publishing processes.

Various workshops with the support of international publishers have been able to inform the young researchers and writers to overcome the language fear as well as barrier. What facilities are available to them are informed in these workshops. The young authors are encouraged to go through the various guidelines what make their writings accepted and appreciated. Various aspects such as components of papers/ articles, kinds of academic publications, ethics in research and of course the copyright aspects have been the concerns in these workshops. Minor aspects also are very significant which include the writing of covering letter as well as the assimilation of thoughts to highlight the originality in research.

The next learning experience was the "Elsevier Science Author Workshop" which was the joint venture of Central Library and School of Life Sciences, JNU in association with Elsevier Science during September 2012. This learning experience had the single object to make the researchers learn how about the research writing for the international journals in their subject fields. Since the early researchers usually belong to class of unaware enthusiast and they need to learn about technical aspects of writing a research paper and the requirements of journal specifically in which a student wishes to submit. Another workshop "Wiley Author Workshop" aimed to support the learners into becoming successful authors as well as publisher of their research. There had been author workshops with a number of publishers such as Emerald Group Publishing Limited, Globe publication Pvt. Limited, Taylor and Francis Group and Kaufman Wills Fusting & Company also.

The "Capacity Building on Digitization" was organized with along with the "Association of Media Libraries and Archives", supported by UNESCO. The digitization and organization of data demands more attention from the library staff. A practical learning sessions on 'Data Curation in the University: Libraries, Research, and Learning' has been informative for the library staff and other library professionals. The presence of cyber-infrastructure as well as "Big Data" has created a different perspective for the research process. There is need to understand and apply the computation, analysis among the professionals. Such learning programs support the academic libraries. The persons in authoritative and technical positions in libraries need to focus on data curation etc. The learning about the data curation in the "context of institutional repositories"; Databib; research data; and data-enabled cyber-infrastructure imbibes a new wave to bring the libraries in most modernized way. At the same time, 'Workshop on Book Care, Repair and Restoration' inform the library staff to keep the fundamental duties well performed.

Again for the researchers, the workshops for knowledge about plagiarism and reference management are significant. Use of reference manager is helpful in the cumbersome process of reference arrangement in the research progress. The free reference management tools are available and the knowledge of using such tools can be supportive to research. The process of taking notes, citing and creating bibliographies is very useful along with the knowledge of collaborating with other researchers and how to discover new research? The scholarly word is facing problems of plagiarism. The workshops on reference management and plagiarism avoidance have the objectives to inform the researchers.

The end of the year 2014 witnessed the workshop on 'Digitization, Digitization Project Management and Digital Archiving'. This workshop was meant for librarians. It was organized by Central Library, Jawaharlal Nehru University, New Delhi in association with IFLA Newspapers Section and Association of Media Libraries and Archives (AMLA) with the objective to train the fellow professionals.

BOOK EXHIBITION

The first book exhibition was held in context with 'Sahitya Akademi' when the year 2013 was about to end. The book exhibition programs were quite interactive and these programs facilitated the showcase of library's treasures. Another exhibition of books, news clippings and articles on Sardar Patel was held approximately one year later. This exhibition of Books, News clippings and Articles was on and about Saradar Vallabhbhai Patel and his contribution to National Unity. The last book exhibition was "Exhibition-cum-sale of Akademi books" in 24 Indian languages on attractive discount by Sahitya Akademi. The following table displays the book exhibitions organized by the Central Library.

Table 6

Title
Exhibition-cum-sale of Akademi books in 24 Indian languages
Exhibition of Books, Newsclippings and articles on Sardar Patel
Sahitya Akademi

(***Source:*** JNU Library Website. http://lib.jnu.ac.in/)

JNU FORUM FOR MUTUAL LEARNING

This forum has been created keeping in view the curious minds of students. It gives an opportunity to students to share knowledge by conducting learning sessions for other students of different subject fields. The JNU Forum for Mutual Learning provides 'an opportunity to know about that particular field may again invoke the interest'. The Forum provides opportunities to students, researchers, faculty and other academic staff. The announcement of the events is made through various means such as JNU Website, social media such as Face book, and the Blog created for the Forum.

The structure of JNU Forum for Mutual Learning consists of Advisory Committee, Conveners, Secretaries and School/ Centre Representative. JNU Forum for Mutual Learning has been very active and it has organized learning sessions for the academic benefits of students and researchers.

REFERENCES

1. Belinda Tiffen & Ashley England. Engaging with clients and personalizing services at UTS Library: measuring the value for libraries and their clients. The Australian Library Journal, Volume 60, Issue 3, August 2011, pages 237-247

2. Brent S. Roberts , Cheryl L. Hoover , (2014) "Waging a successful library funding campaign: a case study", Library Management, Vol. 35 Iss: 3, pp.164 - 174
3. Brian Doherty & Alison Piper. Creating a New Organizational Structure for a Small Academic Library: The Merging of Technical Services and Access Services. Technical Services Quarterly, Volume 32, Issue 2, April 2015, pages 160-172
4. Chérifa Boukacem, (2003) "Inter library loan services and access to electronic resources in French university libraries: a marriage of reason", Interlending & Document Supply, Vol. 31 Iss: 4, pp.218 - 227
5. David Baker, (1987) "Training and Education of Technicians and Assistants in Library Work", Library Management, Vol. 8 Iss: 6, pp.2 - 72
6. Denise Troll Covey, (2002) "Academic library assessment: new duties and dilemmas", New Library World, Vol. 103 Iss: 4/5, pp.156 - 164
7. Dong Hee Shin, Won Yong Kim, Dong Hoon Lee, (2006) "Future public information infrastructure: lessons from four US case studies", info, Vol. 8 Iss: 3, pp.47 - 59
8. Elisabeth Simon, Karl A. Stroetmann, (1998) "Future information infrastructure as a base for the knowledge society a comparison of librarianship in East and West", New Library World, Vol. 99 Iss: 1, pp.20 – 30
9. Graham Matthews, (2003) "Protecting Library Staff, Users, Collections and Facilities: A How To Do It Manual (How To Do It Manuals for Librarians Number 103)", Library Management, Vol. 24 Iss: 3, pp.171 - 171
10. Jennifer E. Nutefall, Faye A. Chadwell, (2012) "Preparing for the 21st century: Academic library realignment", New Library World, Vol. 113 Iss: 3/4, pp.162 - 173
11. JNU Library website. http://lib.jnu.ac.in/
12. Joseph O. Omoniyi, (2002) "The pattern of library utilization by educated *élites* in Nigerian urban centres", Library Review, Vol. 51 Iss: 1, pp.38 - 41
13. Joyce Ray, (2004) "Connecting people and resources: digital programs at the institute of museum and library services", Library Hi Tech, Vol. 22 Iss: 3, pp.249 - 253
14. Jurgita Rudþionienë, Jaroslav Dvorak, (2014) "Public administration approach : What do libraries need for consistent

information services evaluation", Library Management, Vol. 35 Iss: 6/7, pp.495 – 507

15. Karen Calhoun. Technology, productivity and change in library technical services. Library Collections, Acquisitions, & Technical Services, Volume 27, Issue 3, September 2003, pages 281-289
16. Kornelija Petr, Tatjana Aparac Jelusic, (2002) "Public perception of the role and tasks of library and information science professionals in Croatia: an overview of recent activities", New Library World, Vol. 103 Iss: 10, pp.364 - 375
17. Lluís M. Anglada, (2007) "Collaborations and alliances: social intelligence applied to academic libraries", Library Management, Vol. 28 Iss: 6/7, pp.406 – 415
18. Lora Lennertz Jetton & Alberta S. Bailey. The Role of the Access Services Manager in the Virtual Library. Journal of Access Services, Volume 7, Issue 2, March 2010, pages 121-131
19. Mark A. Puente, LaVerne Gray, Shantel Agnew, (2009) "The expanding library wall: Outreach to the University of Tennessee's multicultural/international student population", Reference Services Review, Vol. 37 Iss: 1, pp.30 - 43
20. Michael Lorenzen (2012), Perceptions of Academic Library Development Officers Regarding their Work in Fund-Raising, in Delmus E. Williams, Janine Golden (ed.) *Advances in Library Administration and Organization (Advances in Library Administration and Organization, Volume 31)* Emerald Group Publishing Limited, pp.241 – 289
21. Mohamed Haneefa, (2007) "Application of information and communication technologies in special libraries in Kerala (India)", Library Review, Vol. 56 Iss: 7, pp.603 - 620
22. Prabhjeet Kaur , Paramjeet Kaur Walia, (2015) "Collection development and management within public libraries in Delhi: A study on government owned public libraries in the changing digital environment", Library Management, Vol. 36 Iss: 1/2, pp.99 - 114
23. Richard Levy, (2013) "Library in the Cloud with Diamonds: a critical evaluation of the future of library management systems", Library Hi Tech News, Vol. 30 Iss: 3, pp.9 – 13
24. Robert Newton, (2003) "Staff attitudes to the development and delivery of e learning", New Library World, Vol. 104 Iss: 10, pp.412 - 425
25. Sandra Sharp, (2005) "Fast forward to the future: e enabling in Leeds libraries", The Electronic Library, Vol. 23 Iss: 2, pp.237 – 243

26. S.I. Humbert, E.A. Tilley, (2006) "Redesigning a web site in house to improve information literacy: experiences of a small library", Program, Vol. 40 Iss: 4, pp.346 – 360

27. Sean Cordes, (2008) "Process management for library multimedia development service", Library Management, Vol. 29 Iss: 3, pp.185 - 198

28. Tony Kinder. Learning, Innovating and Performance in Post-New Public Management of Locally Delivered Public Services. Public Management Review, Volume 14, Issue 3, March 2012, pages 403-428

29. Zabed Ahmed S.M. , (2014) "The use of IT-based information services: An investigation into the current status of public university libraries in Bangladesh", Program: electronic library and information systems, Vol. 48 Iss: 2, pp.167 - 184

9
Pervasive Presence of Library and Development of Profession

Various programs and measures conducted, highlighted this library and contributed to the librarianship

INTRODUCTION

The professionalism followed by library is significant in various capacities; such as the internal and external environment as well as how the library is contributing in the organization. The various functions and responsibilities carried out by the library reflect the development inside the library, also outside in the professional arena. The efforts are twofold in that sense, serving the parent organizations and the profession also, to which the entire librarianship belongs. These tasks are supporting the learning process at the campus and the learning by the professionals inside as well as outside the library. The present chapter has taken the aim to highlight various endeavors made by JNU Central

Library, time to time, in order to achieve the success in multifarious capacities.

When the libraries worldwide are observed, their entire years are filled with myriad actions and objectives. The visibility of library is necessary to keep the user informed as well as in the professional environment, a niche that library creates for itself. The library activity calendar is colorful if user visualizes various programs organized by the library, especially at JNU. Since the beginning of year or academic session, the library plans accordingly to make learning better and be professionally active for the library staff too. The library takes care and proliferating its span in terms of services as well as professional development which takes place along with the routine activities, by keeping everyone well informed.

VARIOUS ACTIVITIES AND THEIR EXISTENCE IN NEWS: BE EVERYWHERE AND ANYTIME

When the news spread about the accessibility of JNU library to be in reach 'just a click away', the users of library were delighted as they had now been able to be in touch with an online library called the "Remote Access Services". With the help of remote access the users have access to the following:

a. JNU library catalogue

b. Electronic Books

c. The databases

d. And Electronic Journals

Apart from these resources the users can access more than eight lakh digital news clippings in one go. Since there are number of thesis and dissertations available, this service is very much useful. This facilitates access to more than 20,000 thesis and dissertations. The entire focus was on electronic delivery of information and helping readers to reach every bit of the library collection with the easiest method. The single window access with the feature of just one click away has been a kind of boon to the literature searchers. Where the entire world knows about 'Google', the JNU community was having a platform to access to all e-resources through Web Scale Discovery Services. The simple way of searching the entire library has been an idea like a dream comes true. Just with an institutional e-mail ID (cyber id) and password, the academic community is supported by this single window discovery service.

ONLINE NEWSPAPER CLIPPINGS & NEWS SERVICES

The existence of online newspaper has always been a hi-tech experience for the readers throughout the globe; this became a concern in JNU library also. The provision of online newspapers and online services based on newspapers has become a need in current digital age. The online newspapers and news provisions support the library in providing information without wasting much time. The "newspaper clippings" or "press clippings" involved the digitization of 30 selected newspapers. Now there are more than one million news clippings on various subjects. These subjects have vast coverage of social sciences and international studies. This online news clipping service has been helpful in creating space for other resources and services. The access is obviously very much in vogue and supporting to information services of JNU library.

JNU LIBRARY STRIVES FOR EXCELLENCE

The library is the heart of the university, but to become same it took a leap of vision and understanding the users' needs. The availability of more than six lakh printed books and one lakh e-books available for circulation reflect the richness as well as challenges before the library. There is a history of subscribing to 800 print journals annually from all major international and some Indian publications. In the recent past, the university has access to around 2,300 newspapers from 97 countries in 52 languages, and around 55 research databases. The availability of more than 8 lakh digital newspaper clippings (relevant to 72 subjects) is something the greatest libraries will crave for serving the readers related to various languages. The collection of a rare collection of Urdu, Persian and Art books also enhances the value among the heritage based organization yet there are the chances to have day-today challenge to keep them safe for future generations.

The development of library began with the digitization around 20,000 thesis and dissertations. The only condition of accessing them was to be more than three years old, the other thesis (less than three years old) have been accessible on the intranet anywhere on the campus. The digitization of thesis helped the library to lift its image as well as the usefulness to users also. The progress began with bringing the research output of the university at the surface to be used and valued.

The later days witnessed the organization of workshops, learning sessions for the students to get them published. To keep the originality in research in tact, the procurement of "turn it in" software to check plagiarism has been an achievement. The researchers have now been able to check their research output before submission.

A LIBRARY FOR 24×7

The way the library has been planning to serve the readers in every aspect could be supported by the library; the next step has been the opening doors of library to be operational round the clock. To facilitate reading services more than the office hours schedule, the availability of library premises for the extended hours for the students has been a true friend in the times of examinations, specially. The distinct nature of JNU environment which augments the debating and discussion habits of students, the library has been a great place for the same. The vast collection and a huge number of readers are the honour of a library, at the same time demanding attention to manage efficiently. The popularity of an institution sometimes compel to use stricter means 'control' to have a service scenario unparalleled by any nearby organization. The library implemented an access control system. The registered students are allowed to enter with the ID-cards.

The seating capacity of 128 students has been supportive for the students to come, interact and collaborate with one another. The freedom of expression and choice of reading supported as the JNU library found its role in supporting the very idea of the expression. The library witnessed the reading of Tamil writer's banned book held at JNU. The idea of free expression and the penmanship of Perumal Murugan, a Tamil author was brought to vitality in JNU.

JNU LAUNCHES GOOGLE-LIKE SEARCH ENGINE FOR STUDENTS

Equipping the library users with a tool which is time saving and exploring the entire resource collection was a great need from a long time. The tool was supposed to be handy that could enable the access throughout the collection including the e-books and e-newspapers too. The "EBSCO Discovery Service (EDS)" was launched. The huge community finds it "Google-like single window search". The search box functions as a search engine which brings the desire resource from the library's own collections.

The programs of book releases, invited lectures of prominent experts and training programs have always been methods to connect with the users of library. The library keep on informing and updating the user community is another method to connect and reach the users. The library updated and trained the readers well to use the "New York Times Online newspaper". The access to this newspaper was activated for JNU Library Users. How the Group Passes license to access New York Times Online newspaper can be used within the JNU IP addresses range was informed efficiently through the university website.

The teaching and training of library users and the library staff does not end with the formal or informal lectures. The university librarian went ahead to inform the academic community and about the university's access points. Everybody could listen to University Librarian at Radio 96.9 about the "Round the Clock, Anywhere anytime access" to JNU Library through Single Window Search.

ACCESSING THE ADDED RESOURCES AND TRIAL SOURCES

The enhanced access to e-Books on ProQuest ELibrary Platform was a beautiful idea to provide 309 new e-books which have been added to Central Library Collection. The access to the site has been regulated by IP-authentication. To facilitate the readers, Off-Campus Remote Access was been enabled through the eZproxy. Furthermore the e-books from American Library Association (ALA) were made available for JNU Library Users at JNU IP range. Moving further, approximately 364 Titles from ALA have been accessible for the user community. These titles have been supportive to the library staff also. The journey did not end, adding few more steps it reached to the trial access to Sage Research Methods activated JNU Library Users.

THE SCOPE OF SCOPUS

The research publications by JNU Faculty are available in Scopus. The year-wise Research Publications of JNU

Faculty are available at SCOPUS. This database helps in understanding the research output of the JNU faculty in a systematic manner.

ACCESS NATURE PLANTS MAGAZINE ON TRAIL BASIS

The access to Nature Plants Magazine was made available for JNU Library Users at JNU IP range.

ACCESS ELIBRARY SERVICE FROM GOETH INSTITUT (READ GERMAN MINDS 24X7)

To read German Minds 24x7, the JNU central library endeavored to make the Goeth Institut eLibrary available free of charge for one year. The users have been able to access e-books, e-audios and e-papers. By simply registering, the users could access the e-library. This eLibrary is the virtual library of the Goethe-Institut / Max Mueller Bhavan in India. This facility allowed users to borrow digital media for a predetermined period of time. The users were allowed to download on their computer, tablet or the eReader.

All is learning and no-fun-at-learning cannot survive the test of learning. To have little fun while learning was the aim to try the link "Word Of The Day" at JNU Library Home page. The link "Word Of The Day" has been helpful to get Word of the Day, Free Dictionary, and the Day in the History, Quotation of the Day, Spell-Bee, WordHub and many more. In the same direction to have learning for the users, free trial access to eBooks on Linguistics from De Gruyter was arranged.

Whereas the above discussion reflect the various mainstream activities of library to contribute in the academic excellence of the JNU and to provide development in the library profession, particularly; the information given further displays the various activities conducted by Central Library in a systematic chronological order.

The following tables present the various reasons, developments and occasions when JNU library created news and have been in news. These activities can be better termed as the steps towards creation of better library services as well as contributing to professional development in the area of library profession.

Table 1. News

Title
Sage Research Methods trial access activated
Trail Access to Future Science activated for JNU Library
Trail access to Encyclopaedia Britannica India activated till 8th Nov 2015
Trail access to Bloomsbury Collection activated
Visit Trial Resources to access many e-Resources activated for JNU Library Users
Trial access to Keesings World News from 10th Sept to 8th Oct 2015
Trail Access of Keesings World News activated for JNU Library till 8th October 2015
Are we silent victims of plagiarism? : topic of 24th Lecture Series on 21st September 2015
Orientation cum-Training Programme on "URKUND Plagiarism detection tool provided by INFLIBNET" on 21/09/2015
Central Library, JNU welcomes you to the Book Discussion on "RAJKAMAL CHOUDHARY RACHANAWALI" Date :17/09/2015 Time:4:30 PM at Committee Room, Central Library
Financial Times activated on trial basis till 27th Sept 2015 for JNU Library Users
Training/Orientation Program on Assistive Technologies for Visually Challenged Research Scholars & Students
Photos of Book launch of "Diaspora, Culture and Identity" by Prof. Poonam Bala
Central Library JNU, welcomes you to the Book Release function of "Diaspora, Culture and Identity" by Prof. Poonam Bala and launch by General Dr. V.K. Singh, Minister of State for Overseas Indian Affairs and Prof. Sudha Pai, Rector-I, JNU
Central Library is going to organize Orientation Program on Library Resources and Research Support Services : SSS &SAA on 25th, SIS &

SCL&G on 26th , SLL&CS & SCSS on 27th and All Science Schools on 28th Aug

GUIDELINES FOR SUBMISSION OF DIGITAL COPY OF THESIS AND DISSERTATION IN CD/DVDS TO CENTRAL LIBRARY.

JNU stops screening of Muzaffarnagar riots documentary claiming no permission was sought

JNU students to hold 'Education Parliament' at Jantar Mantar

JNU mulling setting up of National Resource Centre for blind

One-day seminar on "Youth and Sustainable Development: Role of Media, Knowledge Networks and Libraries" by UNIC in collaboration with JNU, AMLA and DLA

Forthcoming activity of JNU Forum for Mutual Learning (JNUFOML)

National Convention on LIS education by IASLIC in collaboration with JNU on 31st July, 2015 between 10 am and 4pm at Committee Room, Central Library, JNU, New Delhi

See video "WELCOME TO ETD2015"

Avail the offer of Institutional Membership of BioMed Central (BMC) to JNU

One more feather in cap of Dr. Ramesh C Gaur, University Librarian, JNU

(***Source:*** JNU Library Website. http://lib.jnu.ac.in/)

Table 2. News

Title
Store e-copies of key papers in 'DigiLocker'
Grammarly Software activated for Reserach Scholar of JNU
Photos of cleaning activity of Library surroundings by its Staff
Orientation programme on Single Window Search: EBSCO Webscale Discovery Services,
Even your Wi-Fi can cause cancer
DU, JNU among 4,000 bodies barred from foreign funding
Only 9 Indian universities make it to Times Asia rankings 2015
Focus on changing tech: JNU head
Free trial access to eBooks on Linguistics from De Gruyter till May 31st 2015 activated for JNU Library Users
Access eLibrary Service from Goeth Institut (Read German Minds 24x7)
Try the link "WORD OF THE DAY" at JNU Library Home page
Meet the Author of "Mandate:Will of the People" Dr. Vir Sanghvi on 7th

May 2015
DU, JNU, IIT depts make it to global top 100 list
Access Nature Plants Magazine on trail basis
Research publications by JNU Faculty available in Scopus
Trial access to Sage Research Methods activated JNU Library Users
eBooks from American Library Association (ALA) available for JNU Library Users at JNU IP range
आदिवासी साहित्य के दूसरे अंक का लोकार्पण एवं परिचर्चा
Access e-Books on ProQuest ELibrary Platform
JNU opens admissions for MPhil/PhD courses
JNU students to enact street plays for farmers' cause in Noida
Listen to Dr. Ramesh C Gaur, University Librarian at Radio 96.9
Listen to Mr. Martin Rama, World Bank and Knowledge sharing session on Plagiarism and How to get it published in Academic Journals
New York Times Online newspaper activated for JNU Library Users
EIU Reports of 76 countries available for JNU Library Users

(***Source:*** JNU Library Website. http://lib.jnu.ac.in/)

Table 3

Title
Book Release function of "The Weight of Violence:Religion, Language, Politics" on 11th March 2015
Scholars protest as stipend hike due since 2010
India amongst last surviving zones of linguistic diversity: JNU professor
Local vocal - Biography of a university
Delhi Election 2015: JNU speech on empowering women sparks debate
JNU launches Google-like search engine for its students(Business Standard)
JNU launches Google-like search engine for its students (WN)
JNU launches Google-like search engine for its students (Niti Central)
JNU launches Google-like search engine for its students(News Nation)
JNU launches Google-like search engine for students
JNU launches Google-like search engine for its students(PTI)
JNU launches Google-like search engine for its students (Deccan Herald)
JNU launches Google-like search engine for its students(NewsR)

JNU launches Google-like search engine for its students

Private varsities start external audit of exam scripts

Reading of Tamil writer's banned book held at JNU

JNU offers mahshi, dalgona to takers

Sudden rise of ABVP shocks red bastion

JNU's gift to students: A library that will stay open 24×7

Mahishasur Day observed at JNU

JNU library strives for excellence

Online newspaper clippings & news services for libraries: Experiences in Indian Libraries

JNU library now anytime, anywhere

(***Source:*** JNU Library Website. http://lib.jnu.ac.in/)

The JNU Central Library organized various learning programs for the library staff and other library professionals in the form of conferences, seminars and training programs. The details are listed as following.

Table 4. Seminar/Conferences

Title
One-day seminar on "Youth and Sustainable Development: Role of Media, Knowledge Networks and Libraries" by UNIC in collaboration with JNU, AMLA and DLA
National Convention on LIS education by IASLIC in collaboration with JNU on 31st July, 2015 between 10 am and 4pm at Committee Room, Central Library, JNU, New Delhi
National Seminar on Transforming UNIVERSITY Libraries: JNU Leading the way
One Day National Seminar on Changing Role of Librarians in Digital Era
OPEN ACCESS WEEK 2013 National Conference on Opening up by Closing the Circle: Strengthening Open Access in India
Managing Indian Media Libraries and Archives Challenges, Opportunities and Best Practices
Knowledge Sharing on Sustainable Development
Managing Electronic Theses and Dissertations (ETDs)

(***Source:*** JNU Library Website. http://lib.jnu.ac.in/)

The library has an agenda that is to excel and marching towards supporting the learning. By various functions it has shown at times that the leadership is the quality by which the contemporary librarianship as well as the organizational progress is not beyond the possibility. The threshold of librarianship is extending towards the academic collaborations with the help of information services. The libraries are integral component of every organization where any kind of learning or learning product is the natural outcome. The academic community and libraries are natural partners. The collaboration between them nurtures the very spirit of librarianship that is to serve. The inter institutional partnerships are also growing to enhance the library services everywhere. The current trends under the umbrella of ICT realities are developing an environment as to bringing out the best from the libraries.

REFERENCES

1. Anne C. Barnhart, Andrea Stanfield, (2013) "Bridging the information literacy gap: library participation in summer transition programs", Reference Services Review, Vol. 41 Iss: 2, pp.201 - 218
2. Binh P. Le , (2015) "Academic library leadership in the digital age", Library Management, Vol. 36 Iss: 4/5, pp.300 - 314
3. Elizabeth Kiondo, (2004) "Around the World to: The University of Dar es Salaam Library: Collection Development in the Electronic Information Environment", Library Hi Tech News, Vol. 21 Iss: 6, pp.19 - 24
4. Gabrielle Ka Wai Wong , Victoria F. Caplan , Diana L. H. Chan , Lois M. Y. Fung , K.T. Lam , (2015) "Actively demonstrating library expertise in a research assessment exercise", Library Management, Vol. 36 Iss: 1/2, pp.115 – 126
5. Hannah Gascho Rempel. Services for Graduate Students: A Review of Academic Library Web Sites. Journal of Web Librarianship Volume 4, Issue 1, March 2010, pages 19-35
6. JNU Library website. http://lib.jnu.ac.in/
7. Joyce Ray, (2004) "Connecting people and resources: digital programs at the institute of museum and library services", Library Hi Tech, Vol. 22 Iss: 3, pp.249 - 253

8. Madhuri Tikam, (2011) "Library volunteerism outcomes: what student volunteers expect", Library Management, Vol. 32 Iss: 8/9, pp.552 - 564

9. Moreno Margarita , Xu Anne , (2014) "Innovation during evolution: Document Supply Service digitises library collections", Interlending & Document Supply, Vol. 42 Iss: 1, pp.1 - 6

10. Peter Fernandez , (2015) ""Through the looking glass: envisioning new library technologies" mobile libraries, beyond the Web site", Library Hi Tech News, Vol. 32 Iss: 3, pp.5 - 8

11. Peter X. Zhou, (2009) "Managing change: East Asian libraries in transition", Library Management, Vol. 30 Iss: 6/7, pp.383 - 392

12. Suzie Allard, (2009) "Library managers and information in World 2.0", Library Management, Vol. 30 Iss: 1/2, pp.57 – 68.

10

Epilogue

A Journey in Progress

About the current transitive activities, future plans etc. Where this library has positioned itself after recent years of deliberations, musings and toils!

The future trends are present in the contemporary practices and the mechanisms to meet the users' expectations. The possibilities are enormous; the ventures are quite promising if the current technologies and tools are taken into consideration. The immediate need is to close the gap between the users' needs and the available technology but the high pricing and man power management are few key factors in bridging the gap. Whereas tools like 'Scopus' or 'Grammerly' are popular, the inspired academic community no longer depends on poor management of resources at the library or the obsolete methods of reference arrangement. On a click, where the organizational research output is available or the ranking could be visualized, the contributions of software/databases are equally significant as the research contributions from the organization itself. For example, on trial at JNU Library, 'InCites' is provided for "evaluating the institutional" productivity. This tool is the "customized one" for the organization and the functioning is "citation-based research analytics".

The reading habit and the methods of accessing information are changing at a fast pace. The relationship of users with the library is on the verge of additional change; because now the library acquires kinds of information resources which no longer are limited to be read in physical premises, also the users possess devices to 'read' the content at the places of their choice by accessing information from a far place. Nowhere the lack in respect towards library is in scene, the methods are changing but the need of library is also visible. The role of librarian and library authority especially in the university system runs parallel to the organizational mission. The academic community knows how the library serves under the craftsmanship of a leading library authority. The conception of professional librarianship and its increasing responsibilities are reframed day by day due to the offerings towards the parent organization and in entire serving scenario.

THE PLANNING AND THE FUTURE

The ongoing practices of library such as having inputs of faculty members in collection development, students representation in enriching the subject collection development are few of the examples where the library has kept the force alive to build community relations in the academic ambience. Putting e-resources on trial access before purchasing/acquiring/subscribing is another example of having the opinion of academic community in collection building, also understating the information needs of users on the time-frame basis. The post-graduate level education and research needs are different as well as intertwining. This aspect of information needs when the students are growing in terms of number as well as in their learning spectrum, the diversity of resources and practices in library is inevitable. The trial information sources might change in their number and products as well yet the continuity reflects the need of understanding users' needs and preferences when the budget positions are tight as well as dwindling. The passport to users' satisfaction is the real knowledge of their needs, choices, and making available the information resources. The contemplation leads to better future if done in right direction, the library is no exception.

The strategic plan for embracing the future keeping in few components of academic ecology is the best option. These facets include the academic community with its diverse subject needs, discovery of right information resources with the appropriate kinds of engagements with the library services. To have the right and balanced relations with branch or schools' library and their users helps in shaping the information services. The trends in other libraries, sometimes, give few more ideas and goals. The priorities and concerns take shape accordingly. The library resources and services become the library ambassadors in the hubs of academia. The focus and continuous addressing of users' learning needs involve the identification of kinds of users along with other building blocks of future library system. The technological advancements and their implementation enhance the innovation and expand the role. The dynamic nature of library services ensures vibrant, inspiring and feasible ideas.

THE FUTURE IN HIDDEN; THE FUTURE HAS ARRIVED!

The library always comprehends the success of present efforts but put deliberations into action also for the coming rainy days in the form of new technologies, tools and expectations from the users. Moving from the library automation towards various implementations of automatic identification systems to facilitate users and library staff too has become a necessity. Apart from the improvement in internal functioning of library, the emphasis is to be given in overall achievement of improvement of library as in whole. Usage of tools such as research analytics, development of repositories and staff development convince the present planning that it leads towards the future which is certainly arriving in the form of more tools, technologies and options to explore in favor of academic community. Somehow the planning may differ from the current agenda of inclusive nature. The twisting nature of government policies during each financial plan, allocated funds for universities, several kinds of grants to be utilized in limited and certain time period compel the libraries to plan in advance as well as in hurried manner too. The sudden increase in demand from the users also disturbs the balanced expenditure.

To have innovative services for the library users is the first and foremost action plan. Including the bigger number of research-oriented library services such as Research avenues, supporting the research and development at users' end etc. The ongoing development of institutional repositories of JNU and the implementation of university research and plagiarism policy narrate a story about research ethics. The plans include the development of Research Archive at JNU which will be a comprehensive database of research. Providing the academic and research profiles will support the research. The countrywide research developments and news platform will prove beneficial for the researchers. Such kind of user-oriented services will augment the finding of specific documents. The library is taking another supportive role of a teacher. It will materialize in the form of various interfaces and activities such as library events blog, more research support links and creation of library-research calendar. Working of library with the academic community in mutual spirit will enhance the learning process for the students which may include the facilities for research performance tools and research data management.

LIBRARY TRANSFORMATION

Library transformation begins with the users' driving motivation for innovative place as library where the inspiration and company of like-minded people is sought. The community connection will be on rise once the global library model is diffused to create academic 'mediaspace' in the academic organization. The 'openness' of library increases by 'co-creation' with the academic community. The meeting of information with the networks integrates because of engagement of knowledge society and knowledge facilitators. The transformation of library as a meaningful space is possible by converting into an inspirational learning space. The growth in library environment can be judged by the unusual demands made by the users which may appear in the form of new services, resources or arrangement of them. Since the learning processes the dialogue orientation due to learning needs and users' experiences, the role of library is very accommodating as well as proliferating. The library reforms itself into a 'performance space' in a way that facilitates the innovation and creation of library services according to users' needs.

Due to the service oriented nature, the library offers some control to users in the form of their needs, expectations by designing the services and arranging the information resources (acquisition, inter library loan etc.). A strong focus is required in the area of adaptation of mobile phone based information services, creation of apps, developing wikis, putting more web 2.0, 3.0 applications into services and so on. The continuous need of rethinking of every current situation involves the fusion of both forms of resources and services. These forms are physical as well as digital/virtual. The branding of library is must due to being symbol of academic, social and continuous development. The traffic to library should be increased by both the ways: entry into physical premises and remote access.

A sustainable model for library development has a component in the form of an activity which is about bridging the technology, user and knowledge. A creation emerges from the deconstruction of old traditions if these traditions hamper the development as the time is about movement through the transcendence. The constant change reflects few of the characteristics of global innovation into libraries, where the functionality is defined by flexibility. The partnership between users and library requires renewal and extended competencies. The partnership can be mapped but takes few considerations such as merging of technology, strategy, infrastructure and the community involvement. The broad ownership, competencies and the library brand are few more pillars to be strengthened.

Annexure 1
Access to Visitors

(As and Available at
Source: JNU Central Library: http://lib.jnu.ac.in)

ACCESS TO VISITOR

For the first time visitor, please try to visit the Library between 9 A. M. - 5:00 P.M. on week days. The researchers from outside the University should ensure that they have recommendation letter and the identity card before they can avail the Library facilities and services. The visitors to the Library may access the online resources in the Cyber Library located on the ground floor of the Library.

FLOOR PLAN

Ground Floor

Circulation Counter	Periodicals & Newspaper Reading Hall
Cyber Library	Display of Faculty Publications
Hellen Keller Unit	Current Periodicals Newspaper
Air conditioned Reading Hall I,II,III	New Books arrivals
Air conditioned Faculty Reading Room	Lockers
Reader's Services Desk	Information Desk & Membership Unit

Mezannine Floor

The Mezanine Floor of the Central Library is adjacent to the Reading Hall on the right hand side of Entrance. In this floor the following offices are available

1. University Librarian Office
2. Library Management Section
3. Automation Unit
4. Acquisition Section
5. Periodical Section
6. Collection Management and Maintenance Section

First Floor : Social Science Section - I: Social Sciences Collection. Photocopying, Printing and Binding facility.

Second Floor : Social Sciences Collection.

Fourth Floor : European and Indian Languages collections

Fifth Floor : Afro-Asian Languages collections and Indian Languages collections

Sixth Floor : P.C. Joshi Archives on contemporary History and Textbooks collection

Seventh Floor : Theses and Dissertations collection, ETD archive ,Newspapers Clippings Unit, Arts and Rare Books collection.

Eight Floor : Russian Collection.

Ninth Floor : ETD Lab, E-Learning and Data Centre, Govt., UN & other International Organizations Publications.

Annexure 2

Rules for Cloak rooms and Lockers

(As and Available at
Source: JNU Central Library: http://lib.jnu.ac.in)

RULES FOR CLOAK ROOMS AND LOCKERS

- Lockers are available for Ph. D. scholars on seniority basis in the Central Library. These are assigned to the scholars at the beginning of Monsoon Semester for one academic year.
- Lockers are not transferable.
- Personal items should not be kept in lockers and the Library assumes no responsibility for any item lost or stolen from the lockers.
- The research scholars are allotted only the lockers and not the table beneath the lockers. If the table is vacant, other scholar can use it.
- The scholars are advised to store only those books which are duly checked-out to them.
- The scholar cannot retain/block more than 6 books (checked-out) in his/her locker at a given time.
- Library materials like Reference books, Rare and Arts books, Thesis & Dissertations, loose/bound volumes of Journals should not be stored in the lockers. Any non-circulating library materials or books, which have not been checked-out shall be removed, if found in the lockers.

- The library reserves the right to open any locker if required, to inspect their contents for library materials that have not been checked-out. Any such item found will be returned to their proper locations and in such situation locker facility shall be immediately withdrawn.
- The scholar is required to use his/her personal locker and hand over the duplicate key to the staff in charge of lockers. In case of change of lock, the staff should be immediately informed and duplicate key handed over.
- Book should be placed with their spines facing outwards.

Annexure: 3

Acquisition Policies

(As and Available at
Source: JNU Central Library: http://lib.jnu.ac.in)

ACQUISITION POLICY

Presently JNU Central Library has a fairly comprehensive book procurement procedure. However, it is being felt that the framework needs little bit modifications to make it more efficient and transparent. Therefore, some changes in the present procedure and also some new methods of procurement of books – both print and online have been introduced w.e.f. 10 January 2012. This has been approved by the Library Advisory Committee in its meeting held on 4.1.2012.

BOOK SELECTION

It has been customary for the faculty and students to take part in book selection in the University. The Library staff usually recommends general reference books and those materials not covered by departmental subject categories like books on library and information science etc. Publishers and Vendors are increasingly providing electronic lists of titles available for purchase, printed catalogues and other printed announcements. These are being forwarded to the Schools and Centers from time to time. Besides catalogues, book reviews in important magazines and databases are also a basis for recommending books for the library. The library also circulates reviews of books to the Schools to keep them informed about new publications.

BOOK PURCHASING PROCEDURE

- The Faculty and students can recommend books and other publications for purchase to the Central Library. It is desired that the list of books requisitioned by the Faculty for purchase for each School/Centre be always routed through the respective Deans/Chairpersons. The requisitions of students can be got approved by the concerned faculty and Dean/Chairperson. It will be desirable that books relating to semester courses may be sent in with one clear semester notice.
- The Library would then check for duplication and place the list of recommended books before the Library Advisory Committee (LAC) for its review. Some very urgent requirements of books forwarded by the Deans/ Chairpersons of respective Schools/Centres may be purchased with the approval of Chairperson of the Library Advisory Committee or by circulation to LAC members.
- Once approved by the LAC for purchase, library staff re-checks the library OPAC to eliminate any duplicate orders etc.
- The Library then prepares the final list of books and obtains financial sanction for their acquisition from the Librarian/Rector/Vice-Chancellor as per the financial powers delegated to each authority.
- On the recommendations of the faculty the Library may purchase multiple copies of only those books which are found to be in great demand but not more than five copies of any book are procured.
- The library will change the earlier practice of ordering books through a select list of approved vendors. The Library may now place orders with any well recognised Vendors registered with Federation of Publishers and Booksellers Association in India (FPBSA) and Delhi

State Booksellers & Publishers Association. The discount insisted upon would be a minimum of 20% on the printed/publishers price. The exceptions would be Government publications/institutional publications and nil discount items. Also in some exceptional cases the vendors charge the library for handling on publishers' demand. In case of multivolume books and encyclopedia, efforts may be made to obtain higher discounts. On the basis of service and past records the review of the suppliers will be done on annual basis.

- A system of online ordering of books and purchase of books by Faculty during their visits abroad has been introduced. Whenever, the faculty are in need of books urgently, they may purchase books for the library from online book stores like amazon.com, flipkart.com etc. using their own credit/debit cards after checking with the library about its non-availability and with due certification from the library to that effect. Same procedure of obtaining approval and financial sanction from the appropriate authority will be followed. They may also be authorised to purchase books on official foreign trips in similar way. Such requests may be processed by circulation to LAC. In such procurements discounts may or may not be available. Sometimes courier/postage charges are also included. The faculty may be reimbursed full amount paid on such transactions on the basis of credit/debit card statement and the bill generated through the online transaction.

  Books purchased on Standing Order:

FACULTY PUBLICATIONS

The Library may now purchase three copies of Faculty publications as and when the publications are brought to the notice of the Library. The financial sanction for procuring the same may be obtained from the Librarian/Rector/VC depending upon their financial powers.

GOVERNMENT DOCUMENTS

Though JNU library is designated as a depository library of all Indian government publications, many Government documents do not reach the Library due to various reasons. Since they are immensely useful information sources for research, therefore, all important Indian government publications have been placed on Standing Order. The list of such publications is to be finalized and should be approved by the LAC from time to time

BILL PROCESSING

Once the books are received in the Library along with the bills, the price of each book and discount rates, bank rates are verified by the concerned staff in Acquisition Section. Entry for each book is made in the Accession Register which has all the relevant details of a book like its price, publisher, vendor, year of publication etc. Then the bills are processed for payment with the accession nos. entered against each item. The In-charge, Acquisition Section certifies above procedure before forwarding bill to Accounts. The bills are put up to the Librarian by In-charge, Library Administration for expenditure sanction on the basis of approval by the competent authority. As per the present practice the Library follows the bank rates prevailing on 1st of every month for the bills from 1st to 15th of every month and the bank rate which prevails on the 16th, for the bills from 16th to 30th/31st of the month.

GIFTS

Constraints of space necessitate the library to stop accepting books from any individuals. Books gifted from major institutions and other individuals may be accepted depending on their utility and physical condition.

B. Subscription to Print/e-Journals and online Databases:

- The Schoolwise/Special Centrewise lists of Print/e-Journals are compiled and forwarded to the respective Deans of Schools/Chairpersons of Special Centres before placing them in the Library Advisory Committee meeting.
- Recommendations are received from the various Schools/Centres to subscribe/renew the Print/e-Journals.
- A Negotiations Committee was formed by the Library Advisory Committee to negotiate with the online journals/database dealers about the subscription cost of each database. The tenure of the Committee may be one year with following composition:
  - i. Chairperson, Library Advisory Committee
  - ii. University Librarian (Ex-officio)
  - iii. Finance Officer (Ex-officio)
  - iv. Five-six members from different Schools/Centres
- After obtaining necessary approval and sanction from the competent authority, the Print/e-Journals are subscribed/renewed through the subscription agents keeping in view their past service records. Some Print/e-Journals are also ordered directly from the publishers.
- In case e-resources are not available through any consortium, publishers of e-resources are directly contacted for raising the invoice.
- The Journals are no discount items and under Govt. of India General Financial Rules, no tender needs to be invited for Print/e-Journals subscription.
- The bills are received from the vendors along with the price proof and the proof of exchange rate as which

prevails on the date of remittance to the publisher.

- The payment for Print/e-Journals subscription is made as per the bank exchange rates prevailing on the date of billing.
- The supplementary bills are accepted in case there is rise in price of the Print/e-Journals and exchange rate.
- Each Print/e-Journal is considered as a separate item in itself. The payment for each Print/e-Journals is treated as Advance Payment. The payment is made from the budget head "Journals". For any other head such as Plan Grant/Project Fund etc.

AMENDMENTS

Amendments are done through LAC's in new procurement policy from time to time.

(a) Online Policy for procurement of Online/ E Books

- A system of online ordering of books and purchase of books by Faculty during their visits abroad has been introduced. Whenever, the faculty are in need of books urgently, they may purchase books for the library from online book stores like amazon.com, flipkart.com etc. using their own credit/debit cards after checking with the library about its non-availability and with due certification from the library to that effect. Same procedure of obtaining approval and financial sanction from the appropriate authority will be followed. They may also be authorized to purchase books on official foreign trips in similar way. Such requests may be processed by circulation to LAC. In such procurements discounts may or may not be available. Sometimes courier/postage charges are also included. The faculty may be reimbursed full amount paid on such transactions on the basis of credit/debit card statement and the bill generated through the online transaction.

- If E Books /E- bundles/ Online Modules recommended by different Faculty of various Schools/Centre's the same will put in LAC's for approval with subject to verification of duplicate checking and availability of funds. Once the LAC's approved the list of e books/ e bundles/ online modules, Acquisition section will call the vendors' for pro-forma invoice and same will be placed in LAC Negotiation Committee with quotations/ Pro-forma invoice along with terms and conditions directly with publishers or through authorized Agency. Once the price fixed after negotiations with publishers/ vendors along with terms and conditions by LACNC, the same will get for financial approval from competent authority. After that, the PO will be raised to the Publishers/vendors for supply of these e books/ e modules, online modules along with marc records.

(b) Approval of Rector for urgent requests

- Some urgently requested books recommended by faculty members, research scholars or students with duly forwarded and recommended by the Deans/ Chairpersons of respective Schools/Centre's, the acquisition section takes approval for the same from the Rector & Chairperson, LAC and procure these urgent books from time to time and the same will be intimate in next LAC.

(c) Discount rates approved by Library Advisory Committee for Procuring

New Discount Rates [August, 2012]

Proposed Discount	*Indian Titles*	*Foreign Titles*
Single copy purchase	20% (for All Publications)	20% (for All Publications)
Multiple copies purchase	25% (Indian titles)	22.5% (Foreign titles)
Multi-volume copies/ Handbook(s)	30% (Indian titles)	25% (Foreign titles)

Encyclopaedia	30% (Indian titles)	25% (Foreign titles)
Single copy purchase	Any order above Rs. 5 lacs to single distributor, an additional discount of 5% on total order (to be calculated on LAC approval basis separately for each approval)	

- The above discount rates are effective from LAC-30th April 2012.

(d) Bank conversion rates

- As per the present practice the Library follows the bank rates taking from SBI JNU New Campus prevailing on 1st of week every month for the bills from 1st to 15th of every month and on 3rd week of every month for the bills from 16th to 30th/31st of the month and updating on central library web page simultaneously.

(e) Charging prices if book lost by Library user's approved in LACs minutes

- Regarding the lost/damaged & gifted books, wherever the cost of the book is not printed, the price could be charged determining the reference to the pages contained in the book The following rates would be applicable in all cases as approved by the LAC Meeting held on 4th October, 2013 [5th LAC 2013].

Foreign Publications

Government	*Commercial*
Rs. 240/- Upto 150 Pages	Rs.400/- Upto 150 Pages
Rs. 400/- Upto 300 Pages	Rs.600/- Upto 300 Pages
Rs. 500/- More than 300 Pages	Rs.800/- More than300 Pages

Indian Publications

Government	*Commercial*
Rs.140/- Upto 150 Pages	Rs.240/- Upto 150 Pages
Rs.220/- Upto 300 Pages	Rs.320/- Upto 300 Pages
Rs.280/- More than 300 Pages	Rs.600/- More than 300 pages

The following amendments to Book Procurement Policy, 2012 were made by the Library Advisory Committee Meeting held on 27th August, 2014

1) We already have a provision for procuring the urgent books through credit/debit cards of the faculty for their students and utilization of this facility is rare and research scholars are requesting to procure the urgent books through their credit cards/debit cards and may be reimbursed the actual amount paid including postage and any other charges paid by them for purchasing the books through either Amazon.com or through any other online sources. So this facility may be added to the visually challenged students/M.Phil./ Ph.D. students for procuring the urgent books with the recommendation from the concerned faculty and duly forwarded to their respective chairperson or deans. The reimbursement will be made after submitting the books along with receipts/bills to the Acquisition Section.

2) In case of text book if one copy is available in the Library and it has been issued to Faculty Members, one more copy of the title will be procured immediately for Library Users.

3) The Committee decided to include following points in book Procurement Policy. All books either single or multi volume title having cost of Rs. 30,000/- should have appropriate justification from the recommending faculty/researcher/student and must be duly forwarded by Dean of School/Centre Chairperson.

Annexure 4

Rules & Regulations

(As and Available at Source: http://lib.jnu.ac.in/ Rules_and_Regulation)

RULES & REGULATION

Membership

1. Only JNU Students, Researchers, Faculty and Staff as registered members are allowed to use the Central Library.
2. Members should produce their Library Membership card at the entrance of the Library.
3. A duplicate Library Membership card will be issued on payment of Rs.100/-.
4. The ex-faculty/staff members may be enrolled as members against a security deposit of Rs. 5000/- (refundable) and registration fee of Rs. 1000/- (non-refundable).
5. Some eminent academicians/scholars and other dignitaries may be enrolled as Special members on the recommendations of the Vice-Chancellor, JNU only against a security deposit of Rs. 5000/- (refundable) and registration fee of Rs. 1000/- (non-refundable).

Visitors

1. Consultation facility is available for Research Scholars of other Universities/Institutions for a short period.
2. The Research Scholars should bring recommendation letter from Supervisor/Guide or letter from the concerned Department/Organization.

3. The visiting scholar should bring original and valid photo ID - Passport (Foreign Scholars), and University issued ID (Indian Scholars).

Circulation

1. Books are issued for a fortnight except textbooks which are issued for overnight use only.
2. Text books with more than 2 copies are checked-out after 2:00 p.m to day-scholars only during the examination period.
3. Students can reserve books at the Circulation Counter in case they are already issued.
4. Books in demand may not be renewed.
5. Readers are responsible for books issued against their names.
6. Library reserves the right to recall any issued book even before the due date.
7. The material such as rare books, theses, dissertations, loose issues of periodicals etc. marked for consultation shall not be issued.
8. Borrowers must satisfy about the physical condition of the books before borrowing otherwise they will be held responsible for any damage later or at the time of return.

Overdue charges

1. Textbooks - the overdue charges Rs. 5/- for first fourteen days.
2. General books - the overdue charges 50 paisa per day for first seven days, rupee one for next seven days.
3. After the expiry of fourteen days, for both Textbooks and General books, the defaulter has to pay the price of the latest edition of the book plus overdue charges for the period the book is kept without authorization.

4. Membership shall be suspended for repeated delay in returning the books.

Use of computers/laptops etc

1. Computer in the library premises should be used for academic purposes only.
2. Online chatting/dating, browsing of social networking sites is strictly prohibited. Strict disciplinary action will be taken against the defaulters.
3. Playing games on computers is strictly prohibited in the entire Library premises.
4. Readers must carry their Library Membership card while using the Cyber Library. They must show their ID card on demand.
5. Readers are not allowed to share their Internet access ID and Password with other students.
6. Changing the settings and display of the computers kept in the Library is not permitted.
7. Use of laptops in the cubical systems where computers are already installed is not permitted.
8. Readers should not remove/unplug computer cables/ connections, network cables and other peripherals/ accessories in the library.
9. Personal keyboard, mouse, etc are not allowed inside the Library.
10. Students must take care of their Pen drives, CD/DVD ROMs, mobiles and wallets etc.

General Reading Hall (24x7)

1. The right to use General Reading Hall is exclusively reserved for bonafide members of Central Library, JNU.
2. Members should produce their Library Membership card at the entrance.

3. Readers should not leave bags/books/copies on the table and cannot claim, capture, and reserve seats for future use.
4. The seats are to be used/occupied on the first come first served basis.
5. Capturing/reserving seats for friends/future use is strictly prohibited. Other scholars may remove the bags and books if these are left unattended on the tables.
6. Readers should not scribble on table tops or damage them.
7. Readers should not clutter the table with heaps of books and other reading material.

Use of lockers

1. Lockers are available for Ph.D scholars on seniority basis in the Central Library. These are assigned to the scholars at the beginning of Monsoon Semester for one academic year.
2. Lockers are not transferable.
3. Personal items should not be kept in lockers and the Library assumes no responsibility for any item lost or stolen from the lockers.
4. The research scholars are allotted only the lockers and not the table beneath the lockers. If the table is vacant other scholar can use it.
5. The scholars are advised to store only those books which are duly checked-out to them.
6. The scholar cannot retain/block more than 6 books (checked-out) in his/her locker at a given time.
7. Library materials like Reference books, Rare and Arts books, Thesis & Dissertations, loose/bound volumes of Journals should not be stored in the lockers. Any non-circulating library materials or books, which have

not been checked-out shall be removed, if found in the lockers.

8. The library reserves the right to open any locker if required, to inspect their contents for library materials that have not been checked-out. Any such item found will be returned to their proper locations and in such situation locker facility shall be immediately withdrawn.
9. The scholar is required to use his/her personal locker and hand over the duplicate key to the staff in charge of lockers. In case of change of lock, the staff should be immediately informed and duplicate key handed over.
10. Book should be placed with their spines facing outwards.

Property Counter

1. In case you lost the Property Counter Token, you will have to pay Rs. 50 as fine towards this.

General rules

1. Readers should observe strict silence inside the Library.
2. Use of Mobile phones is not permitted inside the Library premises.
3. Users are not allowed to carry eatables/drinks inside the Library premises.
4. Library membership card is non-transferable.
5. Readers are not allowed to bring their personal books or any printed material (spiral/bound book/ photocopied material) inside the Library.
6. Personal belongings like bags (laptop, shoulder, sling), umbrellas, etc. should be deposited at the Property Counter against a token. These are not allowed inside the Library.

7. In case the property counter token is lost, the deposited article may be claimed with proper identification after producing a written request.
8. Readers are advised not to leave their valuable items like money, passport, credit card etc. at the Property Counter.
9. Marking, scratching, damaging, mutilating, stealing, library materials or property will invite disciplinary action against the defaulters.
10. Readers should not carry books from one floor to another and should leave the books on the reading table after consulting.
11. Readers should not talk or discuss as they may disturb other readers. Reading halls are meant for individual study and research only.
12. Users should not rest or keep their feet on tables, chairs, shelves, etc.
13. The library shall not be responsible for any loss or damage of the personal belongings of the users.
14. Library staff shall not transmit telephone calls or other personal messages to the readers.
15. The Librarian reserves the right to suspend the membership of any member found misbehaving with the library staff or with any other member.

Annexure 5

Library Statistics

(As and Available at
Source: http://lib.jnu.ac.in/library-statistics)

Collection

Books	*e-Books*	*Currently Subscribed Print Journals*	*Currently Subscribed Print+ Online Journals*	*Currently Subscribed Online Journals*	*Currently subscribed Online Databases*	*Currently subscribed Archives*	*Currently subscribed Newspapers*
3.5 lakh (approx)	1 lakh	314	94	597	40		20

Users (As of 2014-15 only)

UG	*PG*	*M.Phil/Ph.D.*	*Faculty members*	*Staff*	*Special Members*
386	860	864	NA	NA	NA

Library Staff

University Librarian	*Deputy Librarian*	*Assistant Librarian*	*Professional Assistant*	*Semi Professional Assistant*	*Technical Assistant*	*Library Attendent*
1	3	12	24	20	1	26

IT Infrastructure

Screen Reader Software	*RFID based Circulation System*	*Library Website*	*Library Management Software*	*Digital Library Software*	*Digital Display Board*	*NAS Storage*	*Braille Printer*
Yes	Yes	Yes	Yes	Yes	Yes	Yes	Yes